Management & Discipline

Activities Featuring Kagan Structures

Lisa Mitchell

Sarah Walas Teed

Lynsy Oswald

Kagan

Kagan Publishing
981 Calle Amanecer
San Clemente, CA 92673
800.933.2667
www.KaganOnline.com

ISBN: 978-1-933445-55-7

Table of Contents

Section 1: Classroom Behavior..........9

Table of Contents

Table of Contents

Table of Contents

Table of Structures

Introduction

Dear Educators,

We hope you find these lessons to be as useful and as engaging as we do. By teaching appropriate behaviors, you will have better behaved students and more quality teaching time. Thank you for teaching our future leaders how to be respectful to others and to themselves. As educators, we don't always get to see the payoff of what we do, but trust and keep faith that we are making the world a better place by investing in the lives of children. YOU make a difference! We understand how hard your job is each day, but we are thankful for you. Keep up the great work!

We would like to thank the Moline-Coal Valley School District for supporting Kagan Cooperative Learning. The students in Moline-Coal Valley are blessed to have administrators who value staff professional development and have invested in the importance of cooperative learning. The students are also very fortunate to have teachers who want their students to be social and engaged while learning. We would also like to thank the staff at Hamilton Elementary School for being awesome coworkers and friends. We feel very thankful to work with the best!

We appreciate Miguel Kagan for his guidance and review of our manuscripts. Thank you Alex Core for making the book come alive with your book designs and cover. Thank you also to Becky Herrington for managing the publication. We enjoyed working with you! Thank you to Ginny Harvey for copy editing, and Erin Kant, your illustrations brought our visions to life! We are so impressed with the entire Kagan team and grateful to have had the chance to work with all of you on this book!

Enjoy!
Lisa, Sarah, and Lynsy

About the Authors

Lisa Mitchell is currently an Instructional Coach for the Moline-Coal Valley School District. She began her career 30-plus years ago as a special education teacher working with students with severe social and emotional disorders. She moved into regular education in 2000 and has taught 1st, 2nd, 3rd, and 4th grade. Lisa started using Kagan Structures in her classroom to help promote positive learning and engagement in her students. She serves as a Kagan Coach for her building. Lisa is married to Paul, who is a Middle School Social Studies teacher. They both love to follow the Red Sox with their son Derek and spend time with their other son Damon and his family, Wendy and granddaughter Elena. In her free time, Lisa loves to read, work out, and travel to warm, sunny places.

Sarah Walas Teed is a school counselor for the Moline-Coal Valley School District. Sarah is a building Kagan Coach and likes using Kagan Structures in her lessons because of the natural ways they build social skills and engagement. These lessons are what you will find her teaching in her classroom. Sarah wants to be an advocate for all her students and help every one feel welcomed, appreciated, and successful in their learning. Sarah loves to spend time with her husband Jace (also a school counselor), son Cylus, daughter Seneca, and her parents, siblings, and her husband's family. Her family is also very excited to welcome a new baby on the way! Sarah loves Jesus and wants to give Him the glory in all she does.

Lynsy Oswald is an Assistant Principal for the Moline-Coal Valley School District. She is also a Curriculum and Assessment Specialist for Kids at the Core. Lynsy is currently a Kagan Coach and a Kagan School Trainer in Moline. She is passionate about engaging students and helping them grow as learners and as people. Lynsy lives with her husband Rob, her step-daughter Lily, and her two crazy dogs Bella and Riley. In her free time she loves to travel, walk her dogs, play golf, cheer on Lily, spend time with her niece Maddie and her nephews Blake and Owen, and be with her family. She is thankful for her parents' unconditional love and support.

Classroom Behavior

Classroom Disruptions

RallyTable and Pairs Compare

Purpose

- **To increase positive social behaviors in the classroom**
- **To teach or reteach students what behaviors are needed for an appropriate learning environment**

Group Size

- Pairs (RallyTable) and Teams (Pairs Compare)

Materials

- 1 Classroom Disruptions Worksheet per pair or team
- 1 writing utensil per student

Preteaching

- Ask students to describe the perfect learning environment. Give them Think Time. Then make a short list of descriptors on the board.

- Teach the word, "disruption." Disruption in the classroom is anything that stops or bothers someone else's learning. The opposite of disruption is a calm, quality learning environment. A quality learning environment is where all students can think and work without being bothered.

Activity Overview

In pairs, students take turns generating ideas about disruptions and quality learning environments. Together, students list examples in either the Disruption column or the Quality Learning Environment column. Pairs compare their answers with another pair.

Activity Steps

RallyTable:

1 The teacher announces the topic, *"classroom disruptions"* and passes out the Classroom Disruptions Worksheet to each pair. The teacher tells students that they will generate a list of all the things that students (or teachers) do in the classroom that disrupt learning under the "Disruption" column, and quality learning behaviors under the "Quality Learning Environment" column.

2 The teacher asks students to think about disruptions and quality learning environment and provides Think Time.

3 The teacher announces which student will start the list.

4 Students write an idea in one column and the opposite idea in the other. (For example, pencil tapping is a disruption and quiet pencils are a quality learning environment.) Students pass the paper back and forth to each other after they have made a contribution. (Students may not pass the paper without making a contribution. They may not make more than one contribution at a time.)

5 The teacher calls time.

Pairs Compare:

6 Pairs pair to RoundRobin their answers. For each answer, the face partner in the other pair adds the answer to that pair's list or checks it off if they already had it.

7 As a team of four, they see if they can come up with additional ideas.

Structure Alternatives

- *Jot Thoughts*
- *Talking Chips*
- *AllRecord RoundRobin*

Classroom Disruptions

RallyTable and Pairs Compare Worksheet

Directions: Take turns listing disruptions and quality learning environment behaviors in the appropriate columns.

Disruption	Quality Learning Environment
Example: Daydreaming **Example:** Pencil tapping	**Example:** On-task thinking **Example:** Quiet pencils

Management & Discipline: Activities Featuring Kagan Structures
Kagan Publishing • 800.933.2667 • www.KaganOnline.com

Classroom Disruptions

RoundTable

Purpose

* To increase positive social behaviors in the classroom
* To teach or reteach students what behaviors are needed for an appropriate learning environment

Group Size

* Teams

Materials

* 1 Classroom Disruptions Sorting Mat per team
* 1 set of Disruption or Quality Learning Environment? picture cards per team
* 1 pair of scissors per team
* 1 glue stick per team

Preteaching

* Ask students to describe the perfect learning environment. Give them Think Time. Then make a short list of descriptors on the board.
* Teach the word disruption. Disruption in the classroom is anything that stops or bothers someone else's learning. The opposite of disruption is a calm, quality learning environment. A quality learning environment is where all students can think and work without being bothered.

Activity Overview

In teams, students take turns placing a Disruption or Quality Learning Environment? card in the appropriate column on the Sorting Mat.

Activity Steps

1 Student #1 cuts out the Disruption or Quality Learning Environment? cards to prepare for the activity.

2 Student #2 places the cards in a pile in the middle of the team table.

3 Student #3 picks one card and glues it in the appropriate category on the Classroom Disruptions Sorting Mat. The student states why he or she chose the category for the picture card.

4 Teammates take turns sorting the Disruption or Quality Learning Environment? cards and gluing them onto the Sorting Mat until all the cards are on the Sorting Mat.

Structure Alternatives
* Pass-N-Praise
* RoundTable Consensus

Classroom Disruptions

RoundTable Sorting Mat

Directions: Take turns placing the Disruption or Quality Learning Environment? cards in the Disruption column or the Quality Learning Environment column.

Disruption	Quality Learning Environment
Example: Daydreaming **Example:** Pencil tapping	**Example:** On-task thinking **Example:** Quiet pencils

Classroom Disruptions

RoundTable Cards

Directions: Cut out each Disruption or Quality Learning Environment? card along the dotted lines. Place each card in the appropriate column on the Classroom Disruptions Sorting Mat.

① Disruption or Quality Learning Environment?

Praising each other

RoundTable

② Disruption or Quality Learning Environment?

Telling secrets

RoundTable

③ Disruption or Quality Learning Environment?

Interrupting out loud

RoundTable

④ Disruption or Quality Learning Environment?

Quietly studying

RoundTable

⑤ Disruption or Quality Learning Environment?

Annoying a classmate

RoundTable

⑥ Disruption or Quality Learning Environment?

Sharing ideas in a pair

RoundTable

Classroom Disruptions

RoundTable Cards

Directions: Cut out each Disruption or Quality Learning Environment? card along the dotted lines. Place each card in the appropriate column on the Classroom Disruptions Sorting Mat.

⑦ Disruption or Quality Learning Environment?

Cheating on a test

RoundTable

⑧ Disruption or Quality Learning Environment?

Playing / not paying attention

RoundTable

⑨ Disruption or Quality Learning Environment?

Shouting at a classmate

RoundTable

⑩ Disruption or Quality Learning Environment?

Yelling across the room

RoundTable

⑪ Disruption or Quality Learning Environment?

Thinking / paying close attention in class

RoundTable

⑫ Disruption or Quality Learning Environment?

Sleeping in class

RoundTable

Kagan Publishing • 800.933.2667 • www.KaganOnline.com

Classroom Disruptions

RoundTable Cards

Directions: Cut out each Disruption or Quality Learning Environment? card along the dotted lines. Place each card in the appropriate column on the Classroom Disruptions Sorting Mat.

13 Disruption or Quality Learning Environment?

Quietly raising a hand to answer teacher questions

14 Disruption or Quality Learning Environment?

Talking while the teacher is talking

15 Disruption or Quality Learning Environment?

Concentrating on writing project

16 Disruption or Quality Learning Environment?

Studying solo

17 Disruption or Quality Learning Environment?

Playing with the phone at desk

18 Disruption or Quality Learning Environment?

Listening to music in classroom

Classroom Rules

Fan-N-Pick Pairs

Purpose

- To review classroom rules with students
- To ensure that all students know the classroom rules

Group Size

- Pairs

Materials

- 1 set of Classroom Rules cards per pair
- 1 class timer

Preteaching

- Classroom rules should have already been taught before doing this activity.

Activity Overview

Partners play a card game to respond to questions about classroom rules. Roles rotate with each new question.

Activity Steps

1 Student #1 fans the Classroom Rules cards and says, *"Pick a card, any card."*

2 Student #2 picks a card, reads the card aloud, and provides 5 seconds of Think Time.

3 Student #1 answers the question from the Classroom Rules cards.

4 Student #2 restates what Student #1 said and then either praises if correct, or tutors if not correct.

5 Students switch roles for each new round.

Structure Alternatives

- *Fan-N-Pick (4 students)*
- *Quiz-Quiz-Trade*
- *Numbered Heads Together*

Classroom Rules

Fan-N-Pick Pairs Cards

Directions: Cut out each card along the dotted lines. Give each pair a set of cards to play Fan-N-Pick Pairs.

---

① Classroom Rules

What do you do if your pencil breaks and you need another pencil?

Fan-N-Pick Pairs

---

② Classroom Rules

If you feel sick and need to go to the nurse, what should you do?

Fan-N-Pick Pairs

---

③ Classroom Rules

The person next to you won't stop talking, and it is making you uncomfortable because you don't want to get in trouble. What should you do?

Fan-N-Pick Pairs

---

④ Classroom Rules

The teacher holds up the quiet signal. What is the quiet signal? What should you do when the teacher holds it up?

Fan-N-Pick Pairs

---

⑤ Classroom Rules

It is time to line up for recess. How should you line up?

Fan-N-Pick Pairs

---

⑥ Classroom Rules

You really need to go to the bathroom. What do you do?

Fan-N-Pick Pairs

---

⑦ Classroom Rules

The tissue box is empty and you need a tissue. What should you do?

Fan-N-Pick Pairs

---

⑧ Classroom Rules

You forgot your homework at home. What is the consequence of this?

Fan-N-Pick Pairs

Kagan Publishing • 800.933.2667 • www.KaganOnline.com

Classroom Rules

Fan-N-Pick Pairs Cards

Directions: Cut out each card along the dotted lines. Give each pair a set of cards to play Fan-N-Pick Pairs.

⑨ **Classroom Rules**

Someone on your team is being mean to another teammate. You have asked him or her to stop, but it continues. What should you do?

Fan-N-Pick Pairs

⑩ **Classroom Rules**

It is time to sit on the carpet. How should you sit? What are the rules for sitting on the carpet?

Fan-N-Pick Pairs

⑪ **Classroom Rules**

It is silent reading time and another student next to you is talking. What should you do?

Fan-N-Pick Pairs

⑫ **Classroom Rules**

You can't find your scissors and you need them to cut out something. What should you do?

Fan-N-Pick Pairs

⑬ **Classroom Rules**

Where in your room are the rules posted?

Fan-N-Pick Pairs

⑭ **Classroom Rules**

What happens in your classroom if you break a rule?

Fan-N-Pick Pairs

⑮ **Classroom Rules**

What do you do if the teacher is working with a small group and you need help?

Fan-N-Pick Pairs

⑯ **Classroom Rules**

What are ways to celebrate positive behavior choices in your classroom?

Fan-N-Pick Pairs

Classroom Rules

Fan-N-Pick Pairs Blank Template

Directions: Use these blank cards to create your own Fan-N-Pick Pairs Classroom Rules cards.

Classroom Rules

Fan-N-Pick Pairs

Classroom Rules

Fan-N-Pick Pairs

Classroom Rules

Fan-N-Pick Pairs

Classroom Rules

Fan-N-Pick Pairs

Classroom Rules

Fan-N-Pick Pairs

Classroom Rules

Fan-N-Pick Pairs

Classroom Rules

Fan-N-Pick Pairs

Classroom Rules

Fan-N-Pick Pairs

Classroom Rules

Fact or Fiction

Purpose

- **To give students the ability to communicate the expected classroom rules so they will be safe and effective learners**

Group Size

- Whole class (teacher directed)
- Teams (student directed)

Materials

- 1 set of Classroom Rules cards per team
- 1 "Fact" and 1 "Fiction" response card per student

Preteaching

- Review your classroom rules (see sample on page 158).
- Teach the words "fact" and "fiction." Practice several easy statements to make sure the class understands how to play.

Activity Overview

Students detect facts that appear false and fictions that appear true about classroom rules.

Activity Steps

Teacher Directed

1 The teacher reads a true or false statement from the Classroom Rules cards.

2 Each teammate makes his or her best guess by holding up a "Fact" or "Fiction" response card indicating if the statement is fact or fiction.

3 The teacher applauds students who answered correctly.

4 The process is repeated.

Student Directed

1 In teams, one student per team stands and reads the statement on the Classroom Rules card.

2 Teammates think and then share their guesses by holding up a "Fact" or "Fiction" response card indicating if the statement is fact or fiction.

3 If correct, the standing student claps for those who are correct.

4 The process is repeated as teammates take turns reading a new card and leading the team through the cards.

Structure Alternative
- *Showdown*

Classroom Rules

Fact or Fiction Response Cards

Directions: Cut out each card along the dotted lines. Give each student one "Fact" and one "Fiction" response card to play Fact or Fiction.

Classroom Rules

Fact or Fiction Cards

Directions: Cut out each card along the dotted lines. Give each team a set of cards to determine if the statement is fact or fiction.

---

1 Classroom Rules

You should raise your hand if you know the answer.

Fact or Fiction

---

2 Classroom Rules

You should sharpen your pencil during silent reading time.

Fact or Fiction

---

3 Classroom Rules

You should start your day with at least two "ready to go" pencils.

Fact or Fiction

---

4 Classroom Rules

You should look at the teacher when he or she is giving directions.

Fact or Fiction

---

5 Classroom Rules

It's OK to look for your library book during math time.

Fact or Fiction

---

6 Classroom Rules

It's OK to leave the room without asking if you have an emergency.

Fact or Fiction

---

7 Classroom Rules

You should stand in line next to your friend when it is time to line up.

Fact or Fiction

---

8 Classroom Rules

Your teacher likes it when you tap your pencil over and over during spelling tests.

Fact or Fiction

Classroom Rules

Fact or Fiction Blank Template

Directions: Use these blank cards to create your own Fact or Fiction Classroom Rules cards.

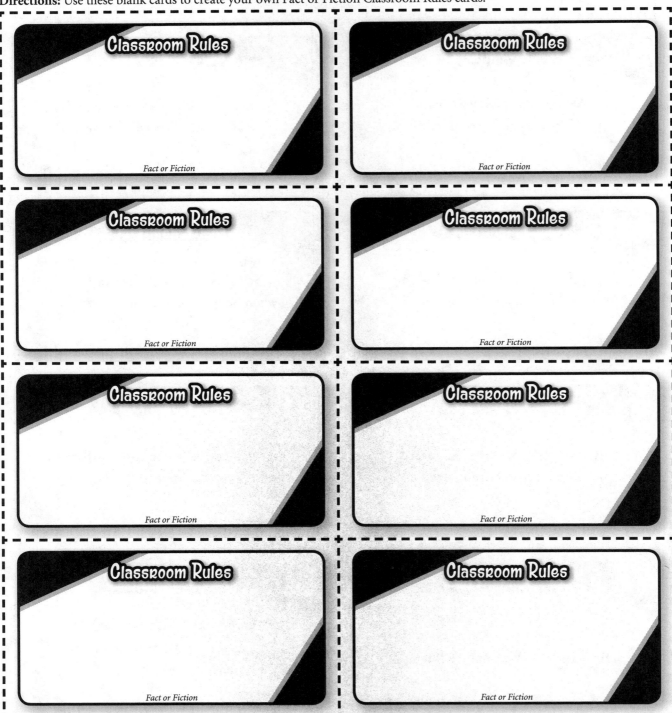

Classroom Rules

Fact or Fiction

Classroom Rules

Fact or Fiction

Classroom Rules

Fact or Fiction

Classroom Rules

Fact or Fiction

Classroom Rules

Fact or Fiction

Classroom Rules

Fact or Fiction

Classroom Rules

Fact or Fiction

Classroom Rules

Fact or Fiction

Classroom Rules

Rappin' Teams

Purpose

- **To build relationships with teammates**
- **To review classroom rules**

Group Size

- Teams

Materials

- 1 Classroom Rules Key Words Recording Sheet per student
- 1 Classroom Rules Rap Rough Draft per team
- 1 Classroom Rules Our Final Team Rap worksheet per team
- 1 writing utensil per student
- 1 class timer

Preteaching

- Classroom rules should have already been taught before doing this activity. This is a review activity.

Activity Overview

Teams develop a rap on classroom rules. They perform their raps for another team.

Activity Steps

1. The teacher assigns the rap topic on classroom rules.

2. Teammates use AllRecord RoundRobin to generate and record a list of eight key words. Teammates take turns starting a key word and everyone records it on the Classroom Rules Key Words Recording Sheet provided.

3. Teammates use AllRecord RoundRobin again to generate and record three or four rhyming words for each key word on the Classroom Rules Key Words Recording Sheet provided.

4. Using the key words, rhyming words, and meter, teammates work together to create lines for their rap using the Rap Rough Draft and then finalize using the Our Final Team Rap worksheet.

5. Teammates practice their rap, deciding roles for each teammate. For examples, which teammates will sing which lines, and which sound effects, clapping, or stomping.

6. Team up—teams perform their rap for another team.

Classroom Rules

Rappin' Teams Key Words Recording Sheet

Directions: Students use this sheet to record the key words and rhyming words for each key word.

Key Words That Go with Classroom Rules	Rhyming Words
①	1. _____ 2. _____ 3. _____
②	1. _____ 2. _____ 3. _____
③	1. _____ 2. _____ 3. _____
④	1. _____ 2. _____ 3. _____
⑤	1. _____ 2. _____ 3. _____
⑥	1. _____ 2. _____ 3. _____
⑦	1. _____ 2. _____ 3. _____
⑧	1. _____ 2. _____ 3. _____

Management & Discipline: Activities Featuring Kagan Structures
Kagan Publishing • 800.933.2667 • www.KaganOnline.com

Classroom Rules

Rappin' Teams Rap Rough Draft

Directions: Teams use this sheet to create rough draft verses for their rap.

Team Rap Rough Draft

Rap Name _____

★ **Key word:** _____
Rap verse using the key word and rhyming word(s): _____
_____
_____
_____

★ **Key word:** _____
Rap verse using the key word and rhyming word(s): _____
_____
_____
_____

★ **Key word:** _____
Rap verse using the key word and rhyming word(s): _____
_____
_____
_____

★ **Key word:** _____
Rap verse using the key word and rhyming word(s): _____
_____
_____
_____

★ **Key word:** _____
Rap verse using the key word and rhyming word(s): _____
_____
_____
_____

Classroom Rules

Rappin' Teams Our Final Team Rap

Directions: Teams use this worksheet to finalize and record their rap. When done writing their rap, they practice it as a team and prepare to perform it.

Team Rap Final Draft

Rap Name _____

_____

_____

_____

_____

_____

_____

_____

_____

_____

_____

_____

_____

_____

_____

Management & Discipline: Activities Featuring Kagan Structures

Kagan Publishing • 800.933.2667 • www.KaganOnline.com

Classroom Behaviors

Showdown

Purpose

- **To increase the safety of all students in the building**
- **To teach or reteach students what is expected in the classroom**

Group Size

- Teams

Materials

- 1 set of Classroom Behaviors cards per team
- 1 "OK!" and 1 "Not OK!" response card per student

Preteaching

- Review your school rules for classroom behavior (see sample on page 159).

Activity Overview

Teams play Showdown to respond to questions about classroom behaviors. Students respond to each question with an "OK!" or "Not OK!" response card.

Activity Steps

1 The teacher selects one student on each team to be the Showdown Captain for the first round.

2 The Showdown Captain draws the top card, reads the statement about classroom behaviors to the team, and provides Think Time.

3 Students independently decide if the behavior is OK or Not OK.

4 When finished, teammates signal they are ready by holding their selected response card against their chest.

5 The Showdown Captain calls, *"Showdown."*

6 Teammates show their response card and discuss why they chose "OK!" or "Not OK!"

7 The Showdown Captain leads the checking.

8 If correct, the team celebrates; if not, teammates tutor, and then they celebrate. If consensus can't be reached with the students, all four hands are raised and the teacher consults.

9 The person on the left of the Showdown Captain becomes the Showdown Captain for the next round.

Note: For younger students, the teacher can be the Showdown Captain and lead the group or class in Showdown.

Classroom Behaviors

Showdown Response Cards

Directions: Cut out each card along the dotted lines. Give each student one "OK!" and one "Not OK!" response card to play Showdown.

Management & Discipline: Activities Featuring Kagan Structures
Kagan Publishing • 800.933.2667 • www.KaganOnline.com

Classroom Behaviors

Showdown Cards

Directions: Cut out each card along the dotted lines. Give each team a set of cards to play Showdown.

---

① Classroom Behaviors

Jack throws a pencil to Eric across the room.

Showdown

---

② Classroom Behaviors

Anna helps Sara pick up her crayon box after it falls.

Showdown

---

③ Classroom Behaviors

Alex laughs at Hannah when she makes a funny face during silent reading time.

Showdown

---

④ Classroom Behaviors

Mark gets up to sharpen his pencil when the teacher is giving directions.

Showdown

---

⑤ Classroom Behaviors

Blake is coloring in his journal during writing time.

Showdown

---

⑥ Classroom Behaviors

Lakyn gives the quiet signal to her teammates when they are working on a math test.

Showdown

---

⑦ Classroom Behaviors

Shanice is looking at the teacher when she is giving directions.

Showdown

---

⑧ Classroom Behaviors

Carmen checks the floor around her desk before she packs up her things.

Showdown

Classroom Behaviors

Showdown Blank Template

Directions: Use these blank cards to create your own Showdown Classroom Behaviors cards.

Classroom Behaviors

Showdown

Classroom Behaviors

Showdown

Classroom Behaviors

Showdown

Classroom Behaviors

Showdown

Classroom Behaviors

Showdown

Classroom Behaviors

Showdown

Classroom Behaviors

Showdown

Classroom Behaviors

Showdown

Compliance

Find Someone Who

Purpose

- To teach students what is expected behavior when they are given a direction by an adult
- To understand compliance is part of being respectful and responsible in class

Group Size

- Pairs

Materials

- 1 Compliance Worksheet per student
- 1 writing utensil per student

Preteaching

- Teach the word "compliance" to students. Compliance is similar to following directions. It is following a reasonable request from an adult within a reasonable time frame. Give several examples of compliance and noncompliance.

Activity Overview

Students play Find Someone Who to respond to questions or statements about compliance.

Activity Steps

1. Students mix in the class, keeping a hand raised until they find a new partner who is not a teammate.

2. In pairs, Partner A asks a question from the Compliance Worksheet; Partner B responds. Partner A records the answer on his or her own Compliance Worksheet and expresses appreciation.

3. Partner B checks and initials the answer.

4. Partner B asks a question about compliance. Partner A responds. Partner B records the answer on his or her own Compliance Worksheet and expresses appreciation.

5. Partner A checks and initials the answer.

6. Partners shake hands, part, and raise a hand again as they search for a new partner.

7. Students repeat Steps 1–6 until their Compliance Worksheets are complete.

8. When their worksheets are complete, students sit down; seated students may be approached by others as a resource.

9. In teams, students compare answers using RoundRobin. If there is a disagreement or uncertainty, they raise four hands to ask a team question.

Compliance

Find Someone Who Worksheet

Directions: Pair up and take turns answering one question. Don't forget to get your partner's initials.

Name _____

①

Compliance

When a teacher says, *"Please raise your hand to speak,"* what should you do before you talk?

_____
_____ [ ] Initials

②

Compliance

If you are told you can play a game after finishing your math paper, what must be done before playing a game?

_____
_____ [ ] Initials

③

Compliance

If your teacher says, *"Work quietly by yourself on an assignment,"* what should another person see and hear when they look at you?

_____
_____ [ ] Initials

④

Compliance

If you are told to stay in the classroom during recess for unacceptable behavior but your friends tell you to go outside anyway, what is the responsible thing to do?

_____
_____ [ ] Initials

⑤

Compliance

If the principal tells you to pick up a milk carton that was left on a lunch table (that isn't even yours!), what is the responsible thing to do?

_____
_____ [ ] Initials

⑥

Compliance

If your teacher sends you to the office to pick up supplies, is it okay to stop by the bathroom? Why or why not?

_____
_____ [ ] Initials

⑦

Compliance

If you ask to go the bathroom and your teacher says, *"Not now,"* what should you say in response?

_____
_____ [ ] Initials

Kagan Publishing • 800.933.2667 • www.KaganOnline.com

Compliance

Find Someone Who Blank Template

Directions: Use this blank worksheet to create your own Find Someone Who Compliance questions.

Name _____

① Compliance

Initials

② Compliance

Initials

③ Compliance

Initials

④ Compliance

Initials

⑤ Compliance

Initials

⑥ Compliance

Initials

⑦ Compliance

Initials

Compliance

Showdown

Purpose

- To teach students what is expected behavior when they are given a direction by an adult
- To understand compliance is part of being respectful and responsible in the classroom

Group Size

- Teams

Materials

- 1 set of Compliance cards per team
- 1 "Smaller" and 1 "Bigger" response card per student

Preteaching

- Tell students it is expected that they follow teacher directions at school the first time the teacher explains what to do.

- Explain that our actions (or how we handle a situation) make the problem either bigger or smaller. Give several examples.

Activity Overview

Teams play Showdown to respond to questions about compliance. Students select either a "Bigger" or "Smaller" response card, indicating whether the behavior will make the problem bigger or smaller.

Activity Steps

1. The teacher selects one student on each team to be the Showdown Captain for the first round.

2. The Showdown Captain draws the top card, reads the statement about compliance to the team, and provides Think Time.

3. Students independently decide if the actions make the problem bigger or smaller.

4. When finished, teammates signal they are ready by holding their selected response card against their chest.

5. The Showdown Captain calls, *"Showdown."*

6. Teammates show their response card and discuss why they chose "Bigger" or "Smaller."

7. The Showdown Captain leads the checking.

8. If correct, the team celebrates; if not, teammates tutor and then celebrate. If consensus can't be reached with the students, all four hands are raised and the teacher consults.

9. The person on the left of the Showdown Captain becomes the Showdown Captain for the next round.

Note: For younger students, the teacher can be the Showdown Captain and lead the group or class in Showdown.

Compliance

Showdown Response Cards

Directions: Cut out each card along the dotted lines. Give each student one "Bigger" and one "Smaller" response card to play Showdown.

Compliance

Showdown Cards

Directions: Cut out each card along the dotted lines. Give each team a set of cards to play Showdown.

---

① Compliance

The teacher tells you to switch to using a crayon on your math paper once the timer goes off. You continue using a pencil.

Showdown

---

② Compliance

The teacher sends you to the office to pick up an important paper. You go directly to the office and then right back to the classroom.

Showdown

---

③ Compliance

During calendar time, the teacher reminds you to keep your hands and feet to yourself. You try really hard to do a better job of keeping your hands and feet to yourself.

Showdown

---

④ Compliance

It is recess time, and you have to miss it because you did not follow classroom rules. You sneak out because you have a guest teacher who won't know you are supposed to miss it.

Showdown

---

⑤ Compliance

You ask to go to the bathroom and the teacher says, *"Not right now."* You scream at the teacher and run out of the classroom.

Showdown

---

⑥ Compliance

The teacher says, *"No markers for this art project."* Even though you really want to use them, you stick with pencil like the teacher said.

Showdown

Compliance

Showdown Cards

Directions: Cut out each card along the dotted lines. Give each team a set of cards to play Showdown.

 Compliance

You are confused about what to write on your paper. You raise your hand and wait for the teacher to come over to help you.

Showdown

 Compliance

During recess, the rule is to not crawl up the slide. You make sure to only go down the slide on your bottom.

Showdown

 Compliance

In the bathroom, the rule is to respect others' privacy. You peek under the stalls to make your friends laugh.

Showdown

 Compliance

It is time for P.E. Your teacher says, *"Line up."* You have a little more work to do on your paper, but you still line up right away.

Showdown

 Compliance

The teacher asks the class to get out their math books. You quickly and quietly get out your math book.

Showdown

 Compliance

Your teacher says to pair up with a partner on your team. You don't want to work with that partner so you refuse.

Showdown

Raising a Hand

Quiz-Quiz-Trade

Purpose

- To make sure all students understand when they need to raise a hand and when they can speak without permission

Group Size

- Pairs

Materials

- 1 Raising a Hand card per student

Preteaching

- Review the expectations for when students need permission to speak.
- Review the expectations of how students signal when they want to speak.
- Give students the sentence stems *"Yes, you need permission because…"* or *"No, you don't need permission because…"*

Activity Overview

The teacher gives each student a Raising a Hand card. Students play Quiz-Quiz-Trade to quiz classmates on whether they need to raise a hand to speak.

Activity Steps

1 The teacher tells students to, *"Stand up, put a hand up, and pair up."*

2 Partner A uses his or her card to quiz Partner B about raising a hand and needing permission to speak.

3 Partner B answers, explaining why or why not you need to raise a hand to speak.

4 Partner A praises if correct or coaches if incorrect.

5 Partners switch roles: Partner B now quizzes Partner A. Partner B praises or coaches.

6 Partners trade cards and thank each other.

7 Repeat Steps 1–6 a number of times.

Structure Alternatives

- *Fan-N-Pick*
- *Inside-Outside Circle*
- *Showdown (with true/false cards)*

Raising a Hand

Quiz-Quiz-Trade Cards

Directions: Cut out each card along the dotted lines. Then fold each card in half so the question is on one side and the answer is on the back. Glue or tape the cards together to keep the answers and questions on opposite sides.

① Raising a Hand Question

Do you need permission to speak?

Yes or No.

Explain why!

Welcome Back to School

Quiz-Quiz-Trade

① Raising a Hand Answer

Yes

Quiz-Quiz-Trade

② Raising a Hand Question

Do you need permission to speak?

Yes or No.

Explain why!

Quiz-Quiz-Trade

② Raising a Hand Answer

No

Quiz-Quiz-Trade

③ Raising a Hand Question

Do you need permission to speak?

Yes or No.

Explain why!

Quiz-Quiz-Trade

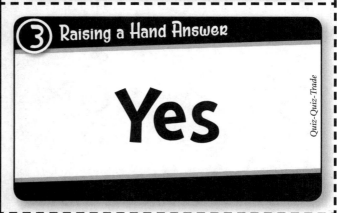

③ Raising a Hand Answer

Yes

Quiz-Quiz-Trade

Raising a Hand

Quiz-Quiz-Trade Cards

Directions: Cut out each card along the dotted lines. Then fold each card in half so the question is on one side and the answer is on the back. Glue or tape the cards together to keep the answers and questions on opposite sides.

④ **Raising a Hand Question**

Do you need permission to speak?

Yes or No.

Explain why!

Quiz-Quiz-Trade

④ **Raising a Hand Answer**

No

Quiz-Quiz-Trade

⑤ **Raising a Hand Question**

Do you need permission to speak?

Yes or No.

Explain why!

Quiz-Quiz-Trade

⑤ **Raising a Hand Answer**

No

Quiz-Quiz-Trade

⑥ **Raising a Hand Question**

Do you need permission to speak?

Yes or No.

Explain why!

Quiz-Quiz-Trade

⑥ **Raising a Hand Answer**

No

Quiz-Quiz-Trade

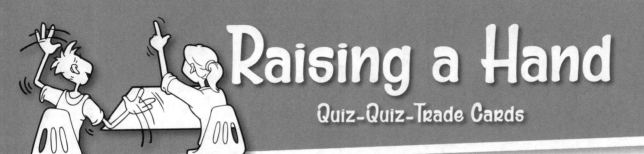

Raising a Hand
Quiz-Quiz-Trade Cards

Directions: Cut out each card along the dotted lines. Then fold each card in half so the question is on one side and the answer is on the back. Glue or tape the cards together to keep the answers and questions on opposite sides.

7 Raising a Hand Question

Do you need permission to speak?

Yes or No.

Explain why!

Quiz-Quiz-Trade

7 Raising a Hand Answer

No

Quiz-Quiz-Trade

8 Raising a Hand Question

Do you need permission to speak?

Yes or No.

Explain why!

Quiz-Quiz-Trade

8 Raising a Hand Answer

Yes

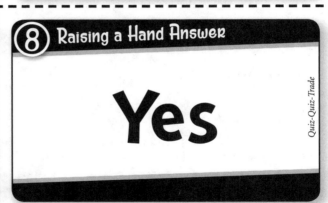

Quiz-Quiz-Trade

9 Raising a Hand Question

Do you need permission to speak?

Yes or No.

Explain why!

Quiz-Quiz-Trade

9 Raising a Hand Answer

No

Quiz-Quiz-Trade

Raising a Hand

Quiz-Quiz-Trade Cards

Directions: Cut out each card along the dotted lines. Then fold each card in half so the question is on one side and the answer is on the back. Glue or tape the cards together to keep the answers and questions on opposite sides.

⑩ Raising a Hand Question

Do you need permission to speak?

Yes or No.

Explain why!

Quiz-Quiz-Trade

⑩ Raising a Hand Answer

No

Quiz-Quiz-Trade

⑪ Raising a Hand Question

Do you need permission to speak?

Yes or No.

Explain why!

Quiz-Quiz-Trade

⑪ Raising a Hand Answer

Yes

Quiz-Quiz-Trade

⑫ Raising a Hand Question

Do you need permission to speak?

Yes or No.

Explain why!

Quiz-Quiz-Trade

⑫ Raising a Hand Answer

No

Quiz-Quiz-Trade

Schoolwide Rules

Our School

Assembly Behavior

Timed Pair Share

Purpose

- To increase positive behavior during schoolwide assemblies
- To encourage problem solving during a presentation or performance

Group Size

- Class or Pairs

Materials

- 1 set of Assembly Behavior cards per class or pair
- 1 class timer

Preteaching

- Review your school rules for behavior at assemblies (see sample on page 159).
- Go over the Assembly Behavior cards with students and share your expectations.

Activity Overview

In pairs, students take turns sharing their responses to questions about appropriate assembly behavior.

Activity Steps

1 The teacher either reads an Assembly Behavior card or Partner A draws a card and reads it aloud to his or her partner. The teacher states that each student will have 20 seconds to share, and then provides Think Time for students to think how they will respond.

2 In pairs, Partner A shares and Partner B listens.

3 Partner B responds with praise.

4 Partners switch roles: Partner B responds to the question, and then Partner A praises Partner B for his or her response.

Structure Alternatives

- *Mix-Pair-Share*
- *Fan-N-Pick*
- *RoundRobin*
- *Talking Chips*

Assembly Behavior

Timed Pair Share Cards

Directions: Cut out each card along the dotted lines. Students share answers to the questions using Timed Pair Share.

 Assembly Behavior

You are at an assembly and the person next to you keeps talking. You have asked him or her to stop once, but the person doesn't. What should you do?

Timed Pair Share

 Assembly Behavior

You have to go to the bathroom while watching an assembly. It is not an emergency. What should you do?

Timed Pair Share

 Assembly Behavior

The boy two rows in front of you is sitting on his knees and you cannot see. What should you do?

Timed Pair Share

 Assembly Behavior

What should you do if you sneeze while at an assembly and you need a tissue?

Timed Pair Share

 Assembly Behavior

What should your body look like while attending an assembly in the gym? Describe it and model it for your partner.

Timed Pair Share

 Assembly Behavior

You just walked into the gym and sat down. The assembly has not yet started. What should you be doing?

Timed Pair Share

 Assembly Behavior

The guest presenter has asked if anyone has any questions. What should you do or say if you have a question?

Timed Pair Share

 Assembly Behavior

When are two appropriate times to clap during a performance? Demonstrate an appropriate clap.

Timed Pair Share

Assembly Behavior

Directions: Use these blank cards to create your own Timed Pair Share Assembly Behavior cards.

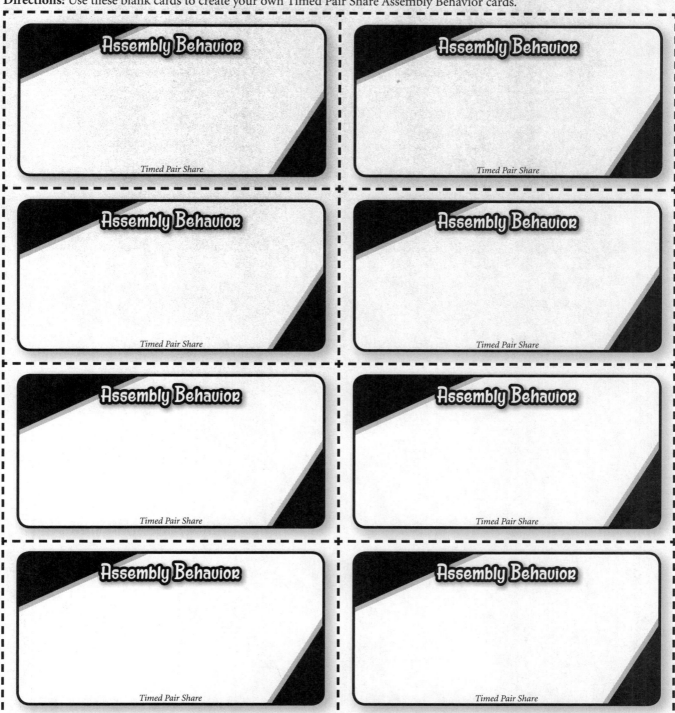

Assembly Behavior	Assembly Behavior
Timed Pair Share	*Timed Pair Share*
Assembly Behavior	**Assembly Behavior**
Timed Pair Share	*Timed Pair Share*
Assembly Behavior	**Assembly Behavior**
Timed Pair Share	*Timed Pair Share*
Assembly Behavior	**Assembly Behavior**
Timed Pair Share	*Timed Pair Share*

Bathroom Behavior

Mix-Pair-Share

Purpose

- To teach or reteach bathroom behavior expectations
- To promote respect, responsibility, and safety in the bathroom

Group Size

- Pairs

Materials

- 1 set of Bathroom Behavior cards per class

Preteaching

- Review your school rules for bathroom behavior (see sample on page 159).
- Teach any new vocabulary words on the matrix that your students might not know (Examples: privacy, stall, or responsible.)

Activity Overview

The class "mixes" until the teacher calls, "Pair." The teacher asks students questions about bathroom behavior and expectations. Students share with their partner and then find a new partner to discuss or answer the teacher's question about bathroom behavior.

Activity Steps

1 The students mix around the room.

2 The teacher calls, *"Pair."*

3 Students pair up with the person closest to them and give a high five. Students who haven't found a partner raise their hands to quickly find each other.

4 The teacher asks a question such as, *"What voice level is expected in the bathroom?",* and gives students Think Time.

5 Students share with their partners using Timed Pair Share.

Structure Alternatives
- *Fan-N-Pick*
- *Numbered Heads Together*
- *Talking Chips*

Bathroom Behavior

Mix-Pair-Share Cards

Directions: Cut out each card along the dotted lines. In pairs, students take turns responding to the question.

---

① Bathroom Behavior

Where do paper towels go when you are finished with them?

Mix-Pair-Share

---

② Bathroom Behavior

What does it mean to use your time wisely in the bathroom?

Mix-Pair-Share

---

③ Bathroom Behavior

What noise should you always hear as someone leaves a bathroom stall?

Mix-Pair-Share

---

④ Bathroom Behavior

What should you do immediately after using the urinal or toilet?

Mix-Pair-Share

---

⑤ Bathroom Behavior

What are the five steps in hand washing?

Mix-Pair-Share

---

⑥ Bathroom Behavior

What voice level is expected in the bathroom?

Mix-Pair-Share

Bathroom Behavior

Mix-Pair-Share Cards

Directions: Cut out each card along the dotted lines. In pairs, students take turns responding to the question.

⑦ **Bathroom Behavior**

When should you go in the bathroom during a bathroom break? When should you stay out?

Mix-Pair-Share

⑧ **Bathroom Behavior**

What are two respectful ways to check to see if a stall is available?

Mix-Pair-Share

⑨ **Bathroom Behavior**

If someone knocks on the stall door that you are using, what should you say to let them know it is in use?

Mix-Pair-Share

⑩ **Bathroom Behavior**

What does privacy mean in the bathroom?

Mix-Pair-Share

⑪ **Bathroom Behavior**

What should you do if you see other students making a mess in the bathroom?

Mix-Pair-Share

⑫ **Bathroom Behavior**

When is it ok to hang out inside the bathroom? When is it not ok?

Mix-Pair-Share

Bathroom Behavior

Mix-Pair-Share Blank Template

Directions: Use these blank cards to create your own Mix-Pair-Share Bathroom Behavior cards.

Bathroom Behavior	Bathroom Behavior
Mix-Pair-Share	*Mix-Pair-Share*

Bathroom Behavior	Bathroom Behavior
Mix-Pair-Share	*Mix-Pair-Share*

Bathroom Behavior	Bathroom Behavior
Mix-Pair-Share	*Mix-Pair-Share*

Kagan Publishing • 800.933.2667 • www.KaganOnline.com

Bathroom Behavior

Numbered Heads Together

Purpose

- To teach or reteach bathroom behavior expectations
- To promote respect, responsibility, and safety in the bathroom

Group Size

- Teams

Materials

- 1 Bathroom Behavior Questions for the teacher (may also be used as a team assignment).
- Numbered Heads Together Kagan software (optional)
- 1 piece of paper or AnswerBoard per student
- 1 writing utensil per student

Preteaching

- Review your school rules for bathroom behavior. (See sample on page 159.)
- Teach any new vocabulary words on the matrix that your students might not know (Examples: privacy, stall, or responsible).

Activity Overview

Teammates put their "heads together" to reach consensus on the team's answer to appropriate bathroom behavior. Everyone keeps on their toes because their number may be called to share the team's answer.

Activity Steps

1 Students number off 1–4 within their teams.

2 The teacher asks a question from the Bathroom Behavior Worksheet and then gives Think Time.

3 Students privately write their answers on paper or an AnswerBoard.

4 The teacher calls, *"heads together,"* and all students lift off of their chairs to show their answers and discuss until the team reaches consensus on an answer.

5 Students sit down when everyone has come to consensus.

6 The teacher calls a number. Students with that number stand. Depending on the question, the teacher instructs students to show their answer, has the class respond chorally, or selects one or more students to respond.

7 Classmates give a cheer and applaud students after answers are read.

8 The teacher repeats the process with the remaining questions.

Structure Alternatives

- *Paired Heads Together*
- *Traveling Heads Together*
- *Stir-the-Class*
- *Mix-Pair-Share*
- *RoundRobin*

Bathroom Behavior
Numbered Heads Together Questions

Directions: In teams, students put their heads together to answer the Bathroom Behavior questions.

Questions about Appropriate Bathroom Behavior

1 What should you do if someone is being unsafe in the bathroom? _____
_____

2 If you see paper towels on the floor, what is the responsible thing to do? _____
_____

3 If someone else forgets to flush the toilet, what is the responsible thing to do? _____
_____

4 When are students in your class allowed to use the bathroom? _____
_____

5 Where can the students look to be reminded about the bathroom rules? _____
_____

6 If people were waiting quietly for a stall, what would that sound like and look like? _____
_____

7 If you bump into someone in the bathroom, what would someone with good manners say?
_____

8 True or false? The bathroom is an appropriate place to talk to your friends about movies, television shows, and sports. _____
_____

9 If someone is goofing around in the bathroom, what words could you use to tell them to stop? _____
_____

10 What is an appropriate number of paper towels to use? _____
_____

Management & Discipline: Activities Featuring Kagan Structures
Kagan Publishing • 800.933.2667 • www.KaganOnline.com

Bathroom Behavior
Numbered Heads Together Blank Template

Directions: Use this blank worksheet to create your own Numbered Heads Together Bathroom Behavior questions.

My Bathroom Behavior Questions

1. _____

2. _____

3. _____

4. _____

5. _____

6. _____

7. _____

8. _____

9. _____

10. _____

HALL PASS

Cafeteria Behavior

Quiz-Quiz-Trade

Purpose

* To make sure all students understand expected cafeteria behavior

Group Size

* Pairs

Materials

* 1 Cafeteria Behavior Statement card per student

Preteaching

* Review the expectations for lunch behavior on your school rules (see sample on page 159).
* Teach the words true and false.

Activity Overview

The teacher gives each student a Cafeteria Behavior Statement card. Students play Quiz-Quiz-Trade to quiz classmates on cafeteria behavior.

Activity Steps

1 The teacher tells students to, *"Stand up, put a hand up, and pair up."*

2 Partner A uses his or her card to quiz Partner B about cafeteria behavior.

3 Partner B answers true or false.

4 Partner A praises if correct or coaches if incorrect.

5 Partners switch roles: Partner B quizzes Partner A. Partner B praises or coaches.

6 Partners trade cards and thank each other.

7 Repeat Steps 1–6 a number of times.

Structure Alternatives

* *Fan-N-Pick*
* *Inside-Outside Circle*
* *Showdown (with true/false response cards)*

Cafeteria Behavior

Quiz-Quiz-Trade Cards

Directions: Cut out each card along the dotted lines. Then fold each card in half so the statement is on one side and the answer is on the back. Glue or tape the cards together to keep the answers and statements on opposite sides.

① Cafeteria Behavior Statement

When sitting in the cafeteria, it is okay to use your outside voice.

Quiz-Quiz-Trade

① Cafeteria Behavior Answer

False

Quiz-Quiz-Trade

② Cafeteria Behavior Statement

If you are not going to eat your grapes, it is okay to throw them at your neighbor.

Quiz-Quiz-Trade

② Cafeteria Behavior Answer

False

Quiz-Quiz-Trade

③ Cafeteria Behavior Statement

Use your manners when talking to the cafeteria staff.

Quiz-Quiz-Trade

③ Cafeteria Behavior Answer

True

Quiz-Quiz-Trade

④ Cafeteria Behavior Statement

When you are done eating, you should throw ALL of your leftover food and wrappers away in the garbage.

Quiz-Quiz-Trade

④ Cafeteria Behavior Answer

True

Quiz-Quiz-Trade

Cafeteria Behavior

Quiz-Quiz-Trade Cards

Directions: Cut out each card along the dotted lines. Then fold each card in half so the statement is on one side and the answer is on the back. Glue or tape the cards together to keep the answers and statements on opposite sides.

5 Cafeteria Behavior Statement

You must stay seated until you are dismissed to line up with your class.

Quiz-Quiz-Trade

5 Cafeteria Behavior Answer

True

Quiz-Quiz-Trade

6 Cafeteria Behavior Statement

It is okay to eat mashed potatoes with your fingers.

Quiz-Quiz-Trade

6 Cafeteria Behavior Answer

False

Quiz-Quiz-Trade

7 Cafeteria Behavior Statement

Singing, screaming, and whistling are not acceptable in the cafeteria.

Quiz-Quiz-Trade

7 Cafeteria Behavior Answer

True

Quiz-Quiz-Trade

8 Cafeteria Behavior Statement

It is okay to make fun of the way other kids eat.

Quiz-Quiz-Trade

8 Cafeteria Behavior Answer

False

Quiz-Quiz-Trade

Cafeteria Behavior

Quiz-Quiz-Trade Cards

Directions: Cut out each card along the dotted lines. Then fold each card in half so the statement is on one side and the answer is on the back. Glue or tape the cards together to keep the answers and statements on opposite sides.

9 Cafeteria Behavior Statement

Making funny faces with your food is okay.

Quiz-Quiz-Trade

9 Cafeteria Behavior Answer

False

Quiz-Quiz-Trade

10 Cafeteria Behavior Statement

Saying, *"please,"* before getting your food from the cafeteria worker is being polite.

Quiz-Quiz-Trade

10 Cafeteria Behavior Answer

True

Quiz-Quiz-Trade

11 Cafeteria Behavior Statement

It is okay to share your milk or juice with your neighbor.

Quiz-Quiz-Trade

11 Cafeteria Behavior Answer

False

Quiz-Quiz-Trade

12 Cafeteria Behavior Statement

Washing your hands before lunch is NOT necessary.

Quiz-Quiz-Trade

12 Cafeteria Behavior Answer

False

Quiz-Quiz-Trade

Cafeteria Behavior

Quiz-Quiz-Trade Cards

Directions: Cut out each card along the dotted lines. Then fold each card in half so the statement is on one side and the answer is on the back. Glue or tape the cards together to keep the answers and statements on opposite sides.

13 Cafeteria Behavior Statement

It is not acceptable to sit on the cafeteria tables.

Quiz-Quiz-Trade

13 Cafeteria Behavior Answer

True

Quiz-Quiz-Trade

14 Cafeteria Behavior Statement

If you need help opening your milk carton you should scream, *"HELP!"*

Quiz-Quiz-Trade

14 Cafeteria Behavior Answer

False

Quiz-Quiz-Trade

15 Cafeteria Behavior Statement

If you wipe your nose with your napkin, ask for another one.

Quiz-Quiz-Trade

15 Cafeteria Behavior Answer

True

Quiz-Quiz-Trade

16 Cafeteria Behavior Statement

If you need to use the bathroom, raise your hand and ask permission.

Quiz-Quiz-Trade

16 Cafeteria Behavior Answer

True

Quiz-Quiz-Trade

Cafeteria Behavior

Quiz-Quiz-Trade Cards

Directions: Cut out each card along the dotted lines. Then fold each card in half so the statement is on one side and the answer is on the back. Glue or tape the cards together to keep the answers and statements on opposite sides.

---

17 Cafeteria Behavior Statement

If something tastes bad, you should not spit it out on the table.

Quiz-Quiz-Trade

17 Cafeteria Behavior Answer

True

Quiz-Quiz-Trade

---

18 Cafeteria Behavior Statement

Running in the cafeteria is **NOT** okay.

Quiz-Quiz-Trade

18 Cafeteria Behavior Answer

True

Quiz-Quiz-Trade

---

19 Cafeteria Behavior Statement

Saying thank you to the cafeteria workers after getting your lunch is **NOT** necessary.

Quiz-Quiz-Trade

19 Cafeteria Behavior Answer

False

Quiz-Quiz-Trade

---

20 Cafeteria Behavior Statement

If your friend forgets to throw away her wrapper, you should leave it on the table.

Quiz-Quiz-Trade

20 Cafeteria Behavior Answer

False

Quiz-Quiz-Trade

Cafeteria Behavior

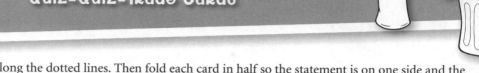

Quiz-Quiz-Trade Cards

Directions: Cut out each card along the dotted lines. Then fold each card in half so the statement is on one side and the answer is on the back. Glue or tape the cards together to keep the answers and statements on opposite sides.

21 Cafeteria Behavior Statement

You must pour your leftover milk in the bucket.

Quiz-Quiz-Trade

21 Cafeteria Behavior Answer

True

Quiz-Quiz-Trade

22 Cafeteria Behavior Statement

If you see a younger student who needs help taking their tray to the table, you should help him or her.

Quiz-Quiz-Trade

22 Cafeteria Behavior Answer

True

Quiz-Quiz-Trade

23 Cafeteria Behavior Statement

If you see trash on the floor, you should pick it up and throw it in the garbage.

Quiz-Quiz-Trade

23 Cafeteria Behavior Answer

True

Quiz-Quiz-Trade

24 Cafeteria Behavior Statement

It is NOT okay to make fun of whatever someone else brought for lunch.

Quiz-Quiz-Trade

24 Cafeteria Behavior Answer

True

Quiz-Quiz-Trade

Cafeteria Behavior

Quiz-Quiz-Trade Cards

Directions: Cut out each card along the dotted lines. Then fold each card in half so the statement is on one side and the answer is on the back. Glue or tape the cards together to keep the answers and statements on opposite sides.

25 Cafeteria Behavior Statement

It is impolite to ask someone else for his or her food.

Quiz-Quiz-Trade

25 Cafeteria Behavior Answer

True

Quiz-Quiz-Trade

26 Cafeteria Behavior Statement

If the cafeteria worker asks you if you want peaches and you do not want them, you should say, "*No, thank you.*"

Quiz-Quiz-Trade

26 Cafeteria Behavior Answer

True

Quiz-Quiz-Trade

27 Cafeteria Behavior Statement

Blowing your milk is rude.

Quiz-Quiz-Trade

27 Cafeteria Behavior Answer

True

Quiz-Quiz-Trade

28 Cafeteria Behavior Statement

Washing your hands before lunch is necessary.

Quiz-Quiz-Trade

28 Cafeteria Behavior Answer

True

Quiz-Quiz-Trade

Kagan Publishing • 800.933.2667 • www.KaganOnline.com

Cafeteria Behavior

Quiz-Quiz-Trade Cards

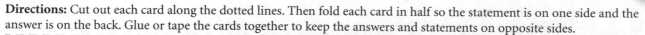

Directions: Cut out each card along the dotted lines. Then fold each card in half so the statement is on one side and the answer is on the back. Glue or tape the cards together to keep the answers and statements on opposite sides.

29 Cafeteria Behavior Statement

Swinging your lunch box is not a safe action.

Quiz-Quiz-Trade

29 Cafeteria Behavior Answer

True

Quiz-Quiz-Trade

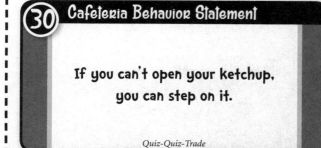

30 Cafeteria Behavior Statement

If you can't open your ketchup, you can step on it.

Quiz-Quiz-Trade

30 Cafeteria Behavior Answer

False

Quiz-Quiz-Trade

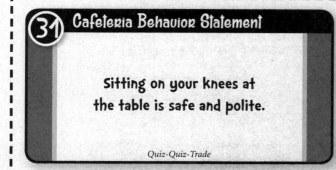

31 Cafeteria Behavior Statement

Sitting on your knees at the table is safe and polite.

Quiz-Quiz-Trade

31 Cafeteria Behavior Answer

False

Quiz-Quiz-Trade

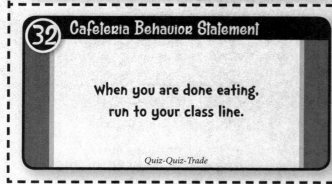

32 Cafeteria Behavior Statement

When you are done eating, run to your class line.

Quiz-Quiz-Trade

32 Cafeteria Behavior Answer

False

Quiz-Quiz-Trade

Hallway Behavior
Showdown

Purpose

- To increase the safety of all students in the building
- To teach or reteach students what is expected in the school hallways

Group Size

- Teams

Materials

- 1 set of Hallway Behavior cards per team
- 1 "OK!" and 1 "Not OK!" response card per student

Preteaching

- Review your school rules for hallway and stairs behavior (see sample on page 159).
- Walk through and identify the quiet zones in the building.
- Model walking on the right side of the hallway/stairs.

Activity Overview

Teams play Showdown to respond to questions about appropriate hallway behavior. Students respond to each question with an "OK!" or "Not OK!" response card.

Activity Steps

1 The teacher selects one student on each team to be the Showdown Captain for the first round.

2 The Showdown Captain draws the top card, reads the statement about hallway behavior to the team, and provides Think Time.

3 Students independently decide if the behavior is OK or not OK.

4 When finished, teammates signal they are ready by holding their selected response card against their chest.

5 The Showdown Captain calls, *"Showdown."*

6 Teammates show their response cards and discuss why they chose "OK!" or "Not OK!"

7 The Showdown Captain leads the checking.

8 If correct, the team celebrates; if not, teammates tutor, and then celebrate. If consensus can't be reached with the students, all four hands are raised and the teacher consults.

9 The person on the left of the Showdown Captain becomes the Showdown Captain for the next round.

Note: For younger students, the teacher can be the Showdown Captain and lead the group or class in Showdown.

Hallway Behavior
Showdown Response Cards

Directions: Cut out each card along the dotted lines. Give each student one "OK!" and one "Not OK!" response card to play Showdown.

Management & Discipline: Activities Featuring Kagan Structures
Kagan Publishing • 800.933.2667 • www.KaganOnline.com

Hallway Behavior

Showdown Cards

Directions: Cut out each card along the dotted lines. Give each team a set of cards to play Showdown.

1 Hallway Behavior

In the lunch line, Evan puts his hands on Steven's shoulders.

Showdown

2 Hallway Behavior

On the way to the bathroom, Stephanie is careful not to bump into anyone.

Showdown

3 Hallway Behavior

José walks with his hands by his side in the hallway.

Showdown

4 Hallway Behavior

George slams his locker because he is mad.

Showdown

5 Hallway Behavior

Sarah hits Lisa because Lisa gave her a mean look in the hall.

Showdown

6 Hallway Behavior

Maria tries to hug Esperanza in the hallway.

Showdown

7 Hallway Behavior

William is trying to whisper to Alondra by the drinking fountain.

Showdown

8 Hallway Behavior

At the drinking fountain, Jace keeps his hands and feet to himself and doesn't squish the person in front of him.

Showdown

9 Hallway Behavior

Alan remembers to give line space when walking from his class to P.E.

Showdown

10 Hallway Behavior

While walking into school, all the children turn their voices off at the door.

Showdown

Hallway Behavior

Showdown Cards

Directions: Cut out each card along the dotted lines. Give each team a set of cards to play Showdown.

 11 Hallway Behavior

Standing outside in line in the morning, Quentin swings his book bag around.

Showdown

 12 Hallway Behavior

Kolby walks on the right down the hall so that he doesn't get in anyone's way.

Showdown

 13 Hallway Behavior

Sarah jumps down the stairs to get to class faster.

Showdown

 14 Hallway Behavior

Joey walks down the stairs one at a time in order to be safe.

Showdown

 15 Hallway Behavior

Todd feels squished in line, so he pushes the person in front of him.

Showdown

 16 Hallway Behavior

No one is looking, so Landon runs in the hallway.

Showdown

 17 Hallway Behavior

Before school, Daniel keeps his backpack on his back and his hands and feet to himself while he waits to enter the building.

Showdown

 18 Hallway Behavior

Stephanie makes sure to keep her eyes on the person in front of her in line so that she doesn't bump into anyone or have too much space in line.

Showdown

 19 Hallway Behavior

Kyle plays a game on his phone as he walks through the hallway.

Showdown

 20 Hallway Behavior

Alex jumps on Geno's back when he sees him in the hallway.

Showdown

Hallway and Stairs Behavior

Find Someone Who

Purpose

◆ **To maintain a quiet/calm environment when moving throughout the building**

◆ **To avoid making more work for the custodian**

Group Size

◆ Pairs

Materials

◆ 1 Hallway and Stairs Behavior Worksheet per student

◆ 1 writing utensil per student

Preteaching

◆ Review your school rules for hallway and stairs behavior (see sample on page 159).

◆ Walk through and identify the quiet zones in the building.

◆ Model walking on the right side of the hallway and stairs.

Activity Overview

Students play Find Someone Who to respond to questions or statements about hallway and stairs behavior.

Activity Steps

1 Students mix in the class, keeping a hand raised until they find a new partner that is not a teammate.

2 In pairs, Partner A asks a question from the Hallway and Stairs Behavior Worksheet; Partner B responds. Partner A records the answer on his or her own Hallway and Stairs Behavior Worksheet and expresses appreciation.

3 Partner B checks and initials the answer.

4 Partner B asks a question about hallway and stairs behavior. Partner A responds. Partner B records the answer on his or her own Hallway and Stairs Behavior Worksheet and expresses appreciation.

5 Partner A checks and initials the answer.

6 Partners shake hands, part, and raise a hand again as they search for a new partner.

7 Students repeat Steps 1–6 until their Hallway and Stairs Behavior Worksheets are complete.

8 When their worksheets are complete, students sit down; seated students may be approached by others as a resource.

9 In teams, students compare answers using RoundRobin. If there is a disagreement or uncertainty, they raise four hands to ask a team question.

Hallway and Stairs Behavior

Find Someone Who Worksheet

Directions: Pair up and take turns answering one question. Don't forget to get your partner's initials.

1 What side of the hallway should you walk on?

_____

_____

_____

Initials

2 How should your feet walk in the hallway?

_____

_____

_____

Initials

3 What should your mouth be doing when you walk in the hallway?

_____

_____

_____

Initials

4 What should you do when you pass another class in the hallway?

_____

_____

_____

Initials

5 Where should your hands be when you walk in the hallway?

_____

_____

_____

Initials

6 What should you do if you are traveling in the hallway by yourself and not with your class?

_____

_____

_____

Initials

7 Where should your hands be when you walk on the stairs?

_____

_____

_____

Initials

8 How should you act if you are with a friend in the hallway?

_____

_____

_____

Initials

9 Where should your phone be when traveling in the hallway?

_____

_____

_____

Initials

Hallway and Stairs Behavior

Find Someone Who Blank Template

Name _____

Directions: Use this blank worksheet to create your own Find Someone Who Hallway and Stairs Behavior questions.

Initials	Initials	Initials
Initials	Initials	Initials
Initials	Initials	Initials

Hallway and Stairs Behavior

Mix-Pair-Share

Purpose

* To maintain a quiet/calm environment when moving throughout the building

Group Size

* Pairs

Materials

* 1 Hallway and Stairs Behavior Questions for the teacher (may also be used as a pair assignment).

Preteaching

* Review your school rules for hallway and stairs behavior (see sample on page 159).

* Walk through and identify the quiet zones in the building.

* Model walking on the right side of the hallway/stairs.

Activity Overview

The class "mixes" until the teacher calls, "Pair." The teacher asks students questions about hallway and stairs behavior. Students share with their partner and then find a new partner to discuss or answer the teacher's question about hallway and stairs behavior.

Activity Steps

1 The students mix around the room.

2 The teacher calls, "Pair."

3 Students pair with the person closest to them and give a high five. Students who haven't found a partner raise their hands to quickly find each other.

4 The teacher asks a question such as, "What could happen if we aren't safe on the stairs?", and gives students Think Time.

5 Students share with their partners using Timed Pair Share.

Structure Alternatives
* Fan-N-Pick
* Numbered Heads Together
* Talking Chips

Hallway and Stairs Behavior
Mix-Pair-Share Questions

Directions: The class mixes, students pair up, and each student answers or discusses a question or statement.

Questions about Appropriate Hallway and Stairs Behavior

1 Describe the correct way to move up and down the stairs._____

_____

_____

2 What could happen if we aren't safe on the stairs?_____

_____

_____

3 Describe the correct way to move in the hallways. _____

_____

_____

4 What could happen if we aren't safe in the hallway?_____

_____

_____

5 If I see you in the hallway, what should I observe you doing?_____

_____

_____

6 Describe appropriate line behavior._____

_____

_____

Schoolwide Rules

AllRecord Consensus

Purpose

- To make sure all students understand expected schoolwide rules in all areas covered on the school matrix

Group Size

- Teams

Materials

- 1 Schoolwide Rules Recording Sheet per student
- 1 writing utensil per student

Preteaching

- Review your school rules with the class (see sample on page 159).

Activity Overview

In teams, students take turns stating a school rule. If there is a consensus, all teammates independently write the school rule.

Activity Steps

1 The teacher may break down school rules into different sections such as cafeteria rules, playground rules, etc. The teacher then selects a student on each team to begin.

2 The selected teammate suggests the first school rule.

3 Teammates put thumbs up, down, or sideways to indicate agreement, disagreement, or doubt.

4 If teammates agree, all students write the answer on their own Schoolwide Rules Worksheets. If there is disagreement or doubt, the team discusses the answer until agreement is reached.

5 The process is continued: each student in turn suggests a new school rule RoundRobin style, the team reaches consensus, and then all teammates record the rule.

Structure Alternatives

- *RoundRobin*
- *AllRecord RoundRobin*

Schoolwide Rules

AllRecord Consensus Recording Sheet

Directions: Teammates record ideas on this Schoolwide Rules Recording Sheet.

Schoolwide Rules Recording Sheet

1. _____

2. _____

3. _____

4. _____

5. _____

6. _____

7. _____

8. _____

9. _____

10. _____

Schoolwide Rules Review

Mix-Pair-Share

Purpose

- To maintain a quiet/calm environment when moving throughout the building
- To teach students the behavior expectations for each common area of the school
- To increase consistency when all staff members use a common language

Group Size

- Pairs

Materials

- 1 set of Schoolwide Rules Review cards per class

Preteaching

- If needed, review your school rules with the class (see sample on page 159).

Activity Overview

The class "mixes" until the teacher calls, "Pair." The teacher asks students questions about schoolwide rules. Students share with their partner and then find a new partner to discuss or answer the teacher's question about schoolwide rules.

Activity Steps

1 The students mix around the room.

2 The teacher calls, "*Pair.*"

3 Students pair with the person closest to them and give a high five. Students who haven't found a partner raise their hands to quickly find each other.

4 The teacher asks a question such as, "*When the bell rings at recess, what should you do right away?*", and gives students Think Time.

5 Students share with their partners using Timed Pair Share.

Structure Alternatives
- *Fan-N-Pick*
- *Numbered Heads Together*
- *Talking Chips*

Schoolwide Rules Review

Mix-Pair-Share Cards

Directions: Cut out each card along the dotted lines. In pairs, students take turns responding to the question or statement.

---

① Schoolwide Rules Review

What does the quiet zone mean at our school? Where are the quiet zone areas of our school?

Mix-Pair-Share

---

② Schoolwide Rules Review

What does it mean to use your time wisely in the bathroom? Give an example of someone using his or her time wisely.

Mix-Pair-Share

---

③ Schoolwide Rules Review

What is the quiet signal for our school? What happens when you hear or see it?

Mix-Pair-Share

---

④ Schoolwide Rules Review

Why do all the students need to follow the rules? What happens when they do? What happens when they don't?

Mix-Pair-Share

---

⑤ Schoolwide Rules Review

You are having a problem with a friend out at recess. What is a problem-solving strategy you could try to make things better?

Mix-Pair-Share

---

⑥ Schoolwide Rules Review

When the bell rings at recess, what should you do right away?

Mix-Pair-Share

---

⑦ Schoolwide Rules Review

What is one way you can show respect at our school?

Mix-Pair-Share

---

⑧ Schoolwide Rules Review

Name one thing that a responsible student would do.

Mix-Pair-Share

Kagan Publishing • 800.933.2667 • www.KaganOnline.com

Schoolwide Rules Review

Find Someone Who

No Running

Purpose

- **To make sure all students understand expected schoolwide rules in all areas covered on the school matrix**

Group Size

- Pairs

Materials

- 1 Schoolwide Rules Review Worksheet per student
- 1 writing utensil per student

Preteaching

- Review your school rules with the class (see sample on page 159).
- Review the questions on the Schoolwide Rules Review Worksheet. This is a review activity.

Activity Overview

Students play Find Someone Who to respond to questions or statements about schoolwide rules.

Activity Steps

1 Students mix in the class, keeping a hand raised until they find a new partner that is not a teammate.

2 In pairs, Partner A asks a question from the Schoolwide Rules Review Worksheet; Partner B responds. Partner A records the answer on his or her own Schoolwide Rules Review Worksheet and expresses appreciation.

3 Partner B checks and initials the answer.

4 Partner B asks a question about school rules. Partner A responds. Partner B records the answer on his or her own Schoolwide Rules Review Worksheet and expresses appreciation.

5 Partner A checks and initials the answer.

6 Partners shake hands, part, and raise a hand again as they search for a new partner.

7 Students repeat Steps 1–6 until their Schoolwide Rules Review Worksheets are complete.

8 When their worksheets are complete, students sit down; seated students may be approached by others as a resource.

9 In teams, students compare answers using RoundRobin. If there is a disagreement or uncertainty, they raise four hands to ask a team question.

Schoolwide Rules Review

Find Someone Who Worksheet

Directions: Pair up and take turns answering one question or statement. Don't forget to get your partner's initials.

Name _____

1

Schoolwide Rules Review

Name the after-school routine.

_____

_____

_____

Initials

2

Schoolwide Rules Review

Why is it important to follow school rules?

_____

_____

_____

Initials

3

Schoolwide Rules Review

Explain why we keep our hands, feet, and objects to ourselves.

_____

_____

_____

Initials

4

Schoolwide Rules Review

What does it mean to be safe?

_____

_____

_____

Initials

5

Schoolwide Rules Review

State three playground rules.

_____

_____

_____

Initials

6

Schoolwide Rules Review

Explain expected behavior in the hallway.

_____

_____

_____

Initials

7

Schoolwide Rules Review

Demonstrate the quiet signal.

_____

_____

_____

Initials

Management & Discipline: Activities Featuring Kagan Structures
Kagan Publishing • 800.933.2667 • www.KaganOnline.com

Schoolwide Rules Review

Find Someone Who Blank Template

Directions: Use this blank worksheet to create your own Find Someone Who Schoolwide Rules Review questions.

Name _____

1

Schoolwide Rules Review

Initials

2

Schoolwide Rules Review

Initials

3

Schoolwide Rules Review

Initials

4

Schoolwide Rules Review

Initials

5

Schoolwide Rules Review

Initials

6

Schoolwide Rules Review

Initials

7

Schoolwide Rules Review

Initials

Schoolwide Rules Review

Turn Toss

Purpose

- **To make sure all students understand expected school rules in all areas covered on the school matrix**

Group Size

- Teams

Materials

- 1 set of Schoolwide Rules Review cards per team
- 1 object for tossing per team (small ball, squishy ball, wad of paper)

Preteaching

- Review your school rules with the class (see sample on page 159).
- Review the Schoolwide Rules Review cards. This is a review activity.

Activity Overview

In teams, one teammate reads a question card, and then tosses a small ball or item to a teammate. The catcher must respond to the question or statement. Team members must toss to a different person each time.

Activity Steps

1 The teacher designates who starts with the "ball" and reads the first Schoolwide Rules Review card.

2 The person picks a card, reads the question or statement to the team, and then tosses the ball to a teammate.

3 The teammate catches the ball and answers the question.

4 The student with the ball now picks a new card, reads the question aloud to the team, and then tosses the ball to another teammate to answer aloud.

5 Repeat questioning and tossing until all questions have been asked or time is called.

Note: If teams finish before time is called, they may continue by asking their own questions about schoolwide rules.

Structure Alternative

This structure can be done as a large group (whole class) activity with the teacher (or designated student) asking the questions. The student who answered the last question tosses to a new student after the teacher gives Think Time.

Schoolwide Rules Review

Turn Toss Cards

Directions: Cut out each card along the dotted lines. Give each team a set of cards to play Turn Toss.

---

1 Schoolwide Rules Review

What does it mean to be safe?

Turn Toss

---

2 Schoolwide Rules Review

Name three playground rules.

Turn Toss

---

3 Schoolwide Rules Review

Why is it important
to follow school rules?

Turn Toss

---

4 Schoolwide Rules Review

Why do we need to keep our hands,
feet, and objects to ourselves?

Turn Toss

---

5 Schoolwide Rules Review

Tell the after-school routine.

Turn Toss

---

6 Schoolwide Rules Review

What is the expected
behavior in the hallway?

Turn Toss

---

7 Schoolwide Rules Review

Show/demonstrate the quiet signal.

Turn Toss

---

8 Schoolwide Rules Review

Name three rules for the cafeteria.

Turn Toss

---

9 Schoolwide Rules Review

How are you respectful
to others in the bathroom?

Turn Toss

---

10 Schoolwide Rules Review

How do you show responsibility
in your classroom?

Turn Toss

Schoolwide Rules Review

Talking Chips

Purpose

- To make sure all students understand the school rules

Group Size

- Teams

Materials

- 1–2 Talking Chips per student
- 1 class timer

Preteaching

- Review your school rules with the class (see sample on page 159).

Activity Overview

Teams discuss schoolwide rules. Teammates have Talking Chips to make sure everyone contributes to the team discussion.

Activity Steps

1 The teacher passes out one or two chips to each member of the team and provides one discussion question below or posts them all to facilitate a longer discussion. The teacher sets a timer for an appropriate amount of time, approximately 3–5 minutes.
  1. *"What are examples of students being respectful to others?"*
  2. *"What are examples of students being responsible?"*
  3. *"What are examples of students being respectful to property?"*
  4. *"If you had to teach a new student the rules, what would you say?"*
  5. *"What rules are hard for you to follow at school? How can you improve at following these rules?"*
  6. *"Why is it necessary that we have schoolwide rules?"*

2 Any student begins the discussion, placing a chip in the center of the table.

3 Any student with a chip continues discussing the schoolwide rules question, using his or her chip.

4 When all chips are used, teammates each collect their own chips and continue the discussion using their Talking Chips. Teams are not finished until the timer beeps.

Structure Alternatives

- *RoundRobin*
- *Timed Pair Share*

Schoolwide Rules Review

Talking Chips

Directions: Cut out the Talking Chips. Give each student one or two chips to play Talking Chips.

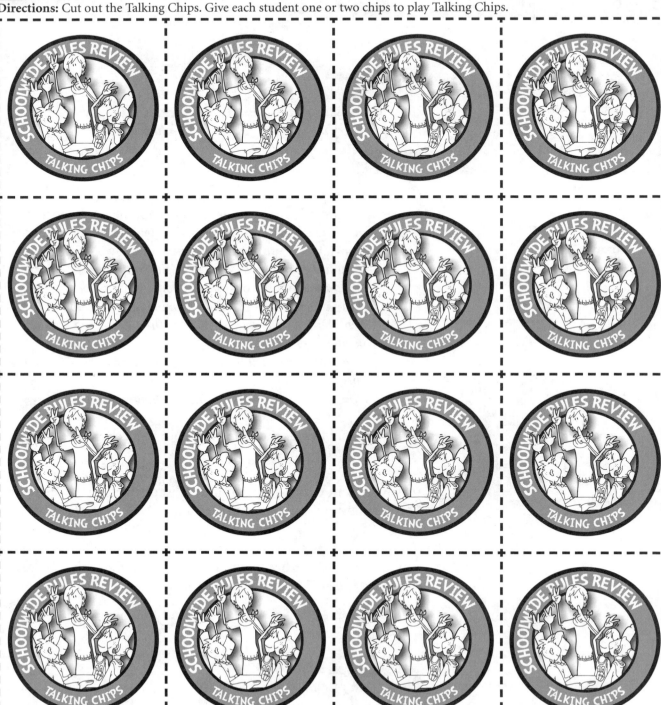

Schoolwide Rules Review

Numbered Heads Together

Thanks for helping me!

Purpose

- To make sure all students understand expected school rules in all areas covered on the school matrix

Group Size

- Teams

Materials

- 1 Schoolwide Rules Review Questions for the teacher (may also be used as a team assignment)
- Numbered Heads Together Kagan software
- 1 piece of paper or AnswerBoard per student
- 1 writing utensil per student

Preteaching

- Review your school rules with the class (see sample on page 159).
- Review the questions on the Schoolwide Rules Review Worksheet. This is a review activity.

Activity Overview

Teammates put their "heads together" to reach consensus on the team's answer to the Schoolwide Rules Review questions. Everyone keeps on their toes because their number may be called to share the team's answer.

Activity Steps

1 Students number off 1–4 within their teams.

2 The teacher asks a question from the Schoolwide Rules Review Worksheet and gives Think Time.

3 Students privately write the answer on paper or an AnswerBoard.

4 The teacher calls, *"heads together,"* and all students lift off of their chairs to show their answers and discuss until the team reaches consensus on an answer.

5 Students sit down when everyone has come to consensus.

6 The teacher calls a number. Students with that number stand. Depending on the question, the teacher instructs students to show their answer, has the class respond chorally, or selects one or more students to respond.

7 Classmates give a cheer and applaud students after answers are read.

8 The teacher repeats the process with the remaining questions.

Structure Alternatives

- *Mix-Pair-Share*
- *Paired Heads Together*
- *RoundRobin*
- *Stir-the-Class*
- *Traveling Heads Together*

Schoolwide Rules Review

Numbered Heads Together Questions

Directions: In teams, students put their heads together to answer the Schoolwide Rules questions or statements.

Schoolwide Rules Review

1 Name three playground rules. _____

_____

2 What is the expected behavior in the hallway? _____

_____

3 Name three rules for the cafeteria. _____

_____

4 Name one way to be respectful to others in the bathroom. _____

_____

5 Name one way to show responsibility in your classroom. _____

_____

6 Name one way to be safe on the stairs. _____

_____

7 What do you use to help others remember to be quiet in the hallway? _____

_____

8 Give one way to show respect at school assemblies. _____

_____

Schoolwide Rules

Swap Talk

Purpose

• To review the school rules
• To build relationships with classmates as a classbuilder

Group Size

• Pairs

Materials

• 1 Schoolwide Rules card per student
• 1 writing utensil per student
• 1 class timer

Preteaching

• This is review; the school rules should have already been taught before doing this activity.

Activity Overview

Students do multiple pairings, each time swapping cards. With each pairing, they each share information on the card they're holding as well as ask each other a question from the card.

Activity Steps

1 Students each receive a Schoolwide Rules card. They respond to what is the most challenging rule for them to follow. They also write a question on the card about school rules.

2 With their completed cards in hand, students stand up, put a hand up, and pair up.

3 Partners take turns sharing the information on their cards and asking and responding to the question.

4 Students swap cards, thank their partner, and put a hand up to find a new partner.

5 With their new partners, students take turns sharing information on the card and asking the question. For example, *"The most challenging school rule for Becky to follow is…"*

6 The process is continued until the teacher calls, *"stop,"* or *"time is up."* With each new pairing, students have a new card with new information and a new question.

Structure Alternatives

• *Timed Pair Share*
• *RoundRobin*

Schoolwide Rules

Swap Talk Cards

Directions: Cut out each Schoolwide Rules card along the dotted lines. Each student receives a card and fills it out to play Swap Talk.

Name _____

★ What is the most challenging school rule for you to follow? Why? _____

_____

_____

_____

_____

★ Question: _____

_____

_____

_____

Name _____

★ What is the most challenging school rule for you to follow? Why? _____

_____

_____

_____

★ Question: _____

_____

_____

_____

Schoolwide Rules Review

Find-the-Fiction

Purpose

♦ To make sure all students understand expected schoolwide rules in all areas covered on the school matrix

Group Size

♦ Teams

Materials

♦ 1 piece of paper per student
♦ 1 writing utensil per student
♦ 1 set of response cards per student

Preteaching

♦ Review your school rules with the class (see sample on page 159).

Activity Overview

Students write three statements about schoolwide rules and read them to teammates. Teammates try to "find" which of the three statements is "fiction."

Activity Steps

1 Teammates write three statements about schoolwide rules on a sheet of paper. Two statements are true and one is false.

2 One student on each team stands and reads his or her schoolwide rules statements to teammates.

3 Teammates are given Think Time to determine which one is the fiction.

4 Teammates select a response card indicating which statement about schoolwide rules is false.

5 Teammates RoundRobin their guesses.

6 The standing student announces the false statement.

7 Students celebrate: The standing student congratulates teammates who guessed correctly. Teammates who were fooled congratulate the standing student.

8 Repeat the process with another teammate.

Structure Alternatives

• **Class Find-the-Fiction:** Find-the-Fiction may be played with the whole class.
• **Fact or Fiction:** Students state either a true or false statement, and it is up to teammates to decide if it is fact or fiction.

Schoolwide Rules Review

Find-the-Fiction Response Cards

Directions: Cut out each response card along the dotted lines. Give each student one set of response cards to display the answer when playing Find-the-Fiction.

Schoolwide Rules Review

#1 Is the FICTION

Find-the-Fiction

Schoolwide Rules Review

#2 Is the FICTION

Find-the-Fiction

Schoolwide Rules Review

#3 Is the FICTION

Find-the-Fiction

Schoolwide Rules Review

RoundTable

Purpose

- To make sure all students understand expected school rules in all areas covered on the school matrix

Group Size

- Teams

Materials

- 1 Schoolwide Rules Review Worksheet for the teacher (may also be used as a team assignment)
- 1 piece of paper per team
- 1 writing utensil per team

Preteaching

- Review your school rules with the class (see sample on page 159).

Activity Overview

In teams, students take turns writing responses to the teacher's question about schoolwide rules.

Activity Steps

1 The teacher asks one question or makes one statement with many possible answers related to schoolwide rules such as, *"List ways to be responsible in the classroom."* More statements and questions are on the Schoolwide Rules Worksheet.

2 Each team has one piece of paper and one pencil that rotate around the team. Each student writes one answer, reads it to the team, and then passes the paper and pencil to the next team member to record an answer.

3 Teams continue passing the team paper, recording a new example until the teacher calls time and asks the next question.

Structure Alternatives

- **Pass-N-Praise:** Students praise the contribution of the person passing the paper to them.
- **RoundTable Consensus:** Students must reach consensus before recording their response.

Schoolwide Rules Review

RoundTable Worksheet

Directions: In teams, take turns passing the paper and pencil, each writing one answer.

Schoolwide Rules Recording Sheet

1 List ways to be safe on the playground. _____
_____
_____

2 List ways to be responsible in your classroom. _____
_____
_____
_____

3 How can you show respect and responsibility in the cafeteria? _____
_____
_____
_____

4 Name the rules for school assemblies. _____
_____
_____
_____

5 How can you be respectful and responsible in the bathroom? _____
_____
_____

6 Name acceptable behaviors for moving through the hallways and on the stairs. _____
_____
_____

Management & Discipline: Activities Featuring Kagan Structures
Kagan Publishing • 800.933.2667 • www.KaganOnline.com

Schoolwide Rules Review

RoundTable Blank Template

Directions: Use this blank worksheet to create your own RoundTable Schoolwide Rules Review questions.

My Schoolwide Rules Questions

1. _____

2. _____

3. _____

4. _____

5. _____

6. _____

7. _____

8. _____

9. _____

10. _____

School Safety Rules

Find Someone Who

Purpose

- To remind students about the importance of safety in school

Group Size

- Pairs

Materials

- 1 School Safety Rules Worksheet per student
- 1 writing utensil per student

Preteaching

- Review the safety expectations for your school and classroom (see samples on pages 158 and 159).

Activity Overview

Students play Find Someone Who to respond to questions or statements about school safety rules.

Activity Steps

1 Students mix in the class, keeping a hand raised until they find a new partner that is not a teammate.

2 In pairs, Partner A asks a question from the School Safety Rules Worksheet; Partner B responds. Partner A records the answer on his or her own School Safety Rules Worksheet and expresses appreciation.

3 Partner B checks and initials the answer.

4 Partner B asks a question about school safety rules. Partner A responds. Partner B records the answer on his or her own School Safety Rules Worksheet and expresses appreciation.

5 Partner A checks and initials the answer.

6 Partners shake hands, part, and raise a hand again as they search for a new partner.

7 Students repeat Steps 1–6 until their School Safety Rules Worksheets are complete.

8 When their worksheets are complete, students sit down; seated students may be approached by others as a resource.

9 In teams, students compare answers using RoundRobin. If there is a disagreement or uncertainty, they raise four hands to ask a team question.

School Safety Rules

Find Someone Who Worksheet

Directions: Pair up and take turns answering one question or statement. Don't forget to get your partner's initials.

Name _____

School Safety Rules ①

Name two ways to be safe on the playground.

_____
_____
_____
_____

Initials [ ]

School Safety Rules ②

What safety rules do you know pertaining to the stairs?

_____
_____
_____
_____

Initials [ ]

School Safety Rules ③

Name two safety rules about coming to school.

_____
_____
_____

Initials [ ]

School Safety Rules ④

Name two safety rules about dismissal.

_____
_____
_____
_____

Initials [ ]

CAUTION CAUTION CAUTION CAUTION CAUTION CAUTION

CAUTION CAUTION CAUTION CAUTION

School Safety Rules ⑤

Why is safety so important?

_____
_____
_____
_____

Initials [ ]

Management & Discipline: Activities Featuring Kagan Structures
Kagan Publishing • 800.933.2667 • www.KaganOnline.com

School Safety Rules

Find Someone Who Blank Template

1 School Safety Rules

Initials

Directions: Use this blank worksheet to create your own Find Someone Who School Safety Rules questions.

Name _____

2 School Safety Rules

Initials

5 School Safety Rules

Initials

3 School Safety Rules

Initials

6 School Safety Rules

Initials

4 School Safety Rules

Initials

7 School Safety Rules

Initials

School Safety Rules

Jot Thoughts

Purpose

- To teach students what the expected behavior is to stay safe at school
- To know how to follow safety rules at school

Group Size

- Teams

Materials

- 10–20 sticky notes or small writing paper pieces per team
- 1 writing utensil per student
- 1 class timer (optional)
- 1 School Safety Rules Brainstorming Mat (optional)
- 1 School Safety Rules Sorting Mat (optional)

Preteaching

- Tell students it is expected that they follow school rules to stay safe at school.
- Give a few examples of ways to be safe at school (Examples: walk in the hallway, sit on your chair, etc.).

Activity Overview

Students each have multiple slips of paper. Teammates "cover the table," writing ideas about school safety rules on their slips of paper.

Activity Steps

1 The teacher names a topic such as ways to be safe at school, sets a time limit, and provides Think Time. (E.g., *"In 3 minutes how many ways can you come up with to stay safe at school?"*)

2 Students write and announce as many ideas as they can in the allotted time, one idea per sticky note or slip of paper. You can use the optional Brainstorming Mat. Students place their sticky notes on the mat as they come up with ideas.

3 After generating ideas, students may sort their ideas into categories. The Sorting Mat is designed for sorting ideas into categories. Students label top of each category.

Note: You can have teams share ideas to compile a classroom list, or teams can share their ideas with other teams.

Structure Alternatives
- *RallyRobin*
- *Talking Chips*

School Safety Rules
Jot Thoughts Brainstorming Mat

Directions: Copy this mat for each team. Write the topic in the center of the mat. Students place sticky notes on the mat as they brainstorm ideas.

Topic

School Safety Rules

Jot Thoughts Sorting Mat

Directions: Copy this mat for each team. Students use it to sort ideas they brainstormed.

_____

_____

_____

_____

Recess Guidelines

Indoor Recess Rules

Find Someone Who

Purpose

* To maintain a safe environment for indoor recess
* To decrease problematic behavior

Group Size

* Pairs

Materials

* 1 Indoor Recess Rules Worksheet per student
* 1 writing utensil per student

Preteaching

* Review your classroom and school rules for indoor recess with your class (see samples on pages 158 and 159).
* Give many examples of what is appropriate and inappropriate.

Activity Overview

Students play Find Someone Who to respond to questions or statements about indoor recess rules.

Activity Steps

1 Students mix in the class, keeping a hand raised until they find a new partner that is not a teammate.

2 In pairs, Partner A asks a question from the Indoor Recess Rules Worksheet; Partner B responds. Partner A records the answer on his or her own Indoor Recess Rules Worksheet and expresses appreciation.

3 Partner B checks and initials the answer.

4 Partner B asks a question about indoor recess. Partner A responds. Partner B records the answer on his or her own Indoor Recess Rules Worksheet and expresses appreciation.

5 Partner A checks and initials the answer.

6 Partners shake hands, part, and raise a hand again as they search for a new partner.

7 Students repeat Steps 1–6 until their Indoor Recess Rules Worksheets are complete.

8 When their worksheets are complete, students sit down; seated students may be approached by others as a resource.

9 In teams, students compare answers using RoundRobin. If there is a disagreement or uncertainty, they raise four hands to ask a team question.

Indoor Recess Rules

Find Someone Who Worksheet

Name _____

Directions: Pair up and take turns answering one question. Don't forget to get your partner's initials.

1
What is an appropriate activity you are allowed to do during indoor recess?

_____

_____

_____

Initials

2
What is something you are NOT allowed to do during indoor recess?

_____

_____

_____

Initials

3
What will happen if you don't follow the rules during indoor recess?

_____

_____

_____

Initials

4
Where should you be during indoor recess?

_____

_____

_____

Initials

5
Is touching other students allowed during indoor recess? Why or why not?

_____

_____

_____

Initials

6
Why is it important to follow the rules for indoor recess?

_____

_____

_____

Initials

7
What is the appropriate voice level for indoor recess?

_____

_____

_____

Initials

8
Is dancing an appropriate activity for indoor recess? Why or why not?

_____

_____

_____

Initials

9
What is appropriate behavior when moving to a different room for indoor recess?

_____

_____

_____

Initials

Management & Discipline: Activities Featuring Kagan Structures
Kagan Publishing • 800.933.2667 • www.KaganOnline.com

Indoor Recess Rules

Find Someone Who Blank Template

Name _____

Directions: Use this blank worksheet to create your own Find Someone Who Indoor Recess Rules questions.

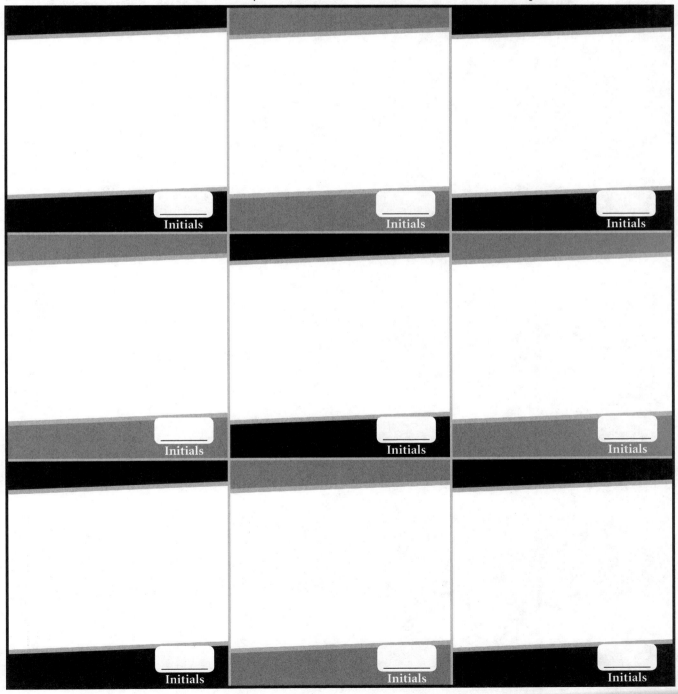

Initials

Initials

Initials

Initials

Initials

Initials

Initials

Initials

Initials

Indoor Recess Rules

Talking Chips

Purpose

◆ To make sure all students understand expected indoor recess rules

◆ To increase safety during indoor recess

Group Size

◆ Teams

Materials

◆ 1–2 Talking Chips per student

◆ 1 class timer

Preteaching

◆ Review your classroom and school rules for indoor recess with the class (see samples on pages 158 and 159).

◆ Generate a list together of specific "Do's and Don'ts" for indoor recess.

Activity Overview

Teams discuss indoor recess rules. Teammates have Talking Chips to make sure everyone contributes to the team discussion on indoor recess rules.

Activity Steps

1 The teacher passes out one or two chips to each member of the team, provides the discussion topic on indoor recess rules, and provides Think Time. The teacher sets a timer for an appropriate amount of time, approximately 3–5 minutes.

2 Any student begins the discussion placing a chip in the center of the table.

3 Any student with a chip continues discussing the indoor recess rules, using his or her chip.

4 When all chips are used, teammates each collect their own chips and continue the discussion using their Talking Chips. Teams are not finished until the timer beeps.

Structure Alternatives

• *RoundRobin*
• *Timed Pair Share*

Indoor Recess Rules

Talking Chips

Directions: Cut out the Talking Chips. Give each student one or two chips to play Talking Chips.

Playground Behavior

RoundTable

Purpose

- **To make sure all students understand expected school rules in all areas covered on the school matrix**

Group Size

- Teams

Materials

- 1 Playground Behavior Worksheet for the teacher (may also be used as a team assignment)
- 1 piece of paper per student
- 1 writing utensil per student

Preteaching

- Review your school rules for playground behavior with the class (see sample on page 159).

Activity Overview

In teams, students take turns writing responses to the teacher's question or statement about playground behavior.

Activity Steps

1 The teacher asks one question or makes one statement with many possible answers related to playground behavior such as, *"List ways to be safe on the playground."* More statements and questions are on the Playground Behavior Worksheet.

2 Each team has one piece of paper and one pencil that rotate around the team. Each student writes one answer, reads it to the team, and passes the paper and pencil to the next team member to record an answer.

3 Teams continue passing the team paper, recording additional ideas until the teacher calls time and asks the next question.

Structure Alternatives

- **Pass-N-Praise:** Students praise the contribution of the person passing the paper to them.
- **RoundTable Consensus:** Students must reach consensus before recording their response.

Playground Behavior

RoundTable Worksheet

Directions: In teams, take turns passing the paper and pencil, each writing one answer.

Playground Behavior Recording Sheet

1 List ways to be safe on the playground. _____
_____
_____
_____

2 List as many different games as you can that can be played on the playground.
_____
_____
_____

3 State the rules for using playground equipment. _____
_____
_____
_____

4 What are things you should NOT do on the playground? _____
_____
_____
_____

5 What are things you should do if someone gets hurt on the playground? _____
_____
_____
_____

6 List games that can be played in teams. _____
_____
_____
_____

7 List games that can be played in pairs. _____
_____
_____
_____

Management & Discipline: Activities Featuring Kagan Structures
Kagan Publishing • 800.933.2667 • www.KaganOnline.com

Appropriate Recess Games

RallyRobin

Purpose

- **To make sure all students understand what games are appropriate for recess**
- **To increase safety and respect at recess**

Group Size

- Pairs

Preteaching

- Review recess games allowed at school.
- Generate a list together of specific "Do's and Don'ts" for games at recess.

Activity Overview

In pairs, students take turns orally listing appropriate recess games.

Activity Steps

 The teacher announces the topic, *"Games we could play at recess,"* and provides Think Time.

 In pairs, partners take turns listing ideas about appropriate recess games.

 This back-and-forth verbal rally continues until the teacher calls time.

Additional Related RallyRobin Topics
- Ball sports
- Board games
- Games you can play alone
- Individual sports
- Indoor games we can play
- Students I could ask to play with at recess
- Places I can play at recess
- Playground rules
- Rules for a sport
- Sports I like to play
- Team sports
- Ways to solve problems at recess

Structure Alternatives
- *Jot Thoughts (write instead of talk)*
- *Talking Chips*

Respecting Teachers

Guest Teachers

Fan-N-Pick

Purpose

- To increase positive behaviors when a guest teacher is in the building
- To teach and remind students what is expected when a guest teacher is in the building

Group Size

- Teams

Materials

- 1 set of Guest Teachers cards per team
- 1 Fan-N-Pick Mat per team (optional)

Preteaching

- Take a few minutes to review your class rules with everyone (see sample on page 158).
- Remind students the rules do not change if a guest teacher is present.

Activity Overview

Teammates play a card game to respond to the questions or statements about guest teachers. Roles rotate with each new question or statement.

Activity Steps

1 Student #1 holds the Guest Teachers cards in a fan and says, *"Pick a card, any card!"*

2 Student #2 picks a card, reads the question or statement aloud, and allows 5 seconds of Think Time.

3 Student #3 answers the question or statement about guest teachers.

4 Student #4 responds to the answer:
- For right or wrong answers, student #4 checks and then either praises or tutors.
- For questions that have no right or wrong answer, Student #4 does not check for correctness, but praises and then paraphrases the thinking that went into the answer.

5 Students rotate roles, one person clockwise for each new round.

Note: A Fan-N-Pick Mat can be placed in the center of the table to lead students through the structure, ensuring everyone keeps actively involved.

Structure Alternatives
- *Mix-Pair-Share*
- *StandUp–HandUp–PairUp*
- *Timed Pair Share*
- *Numbered Heads Together*

Guest Teachers

Fan-N-Pick Cards

Directions: Cut out each card along the dotted lines. Give each team a set of cards to play Fan-N-Pick.

 1 Guest Teachers

Name one thing that is difficult about having a guest teacher.

Fan-N-Pick

 2 Guest Teachers

What consequences do students have if they do not follow the rules when a guest teacher is in the classroom?

Fan-N-Pick

 3 Guest Teachers

Describe appropriate behavior during reading teams when there is a guest teacher.

Fan-N-Pick

 4 Guest Teachers

Describe appropriate behavior during math when there is a guest teacher.

Fan-N-Pick

 5 Guest Teachers

Describe appropriate behavior during silent work time when there is a guest teacher.

Fan-N-Pick

 6 Guest Teachers

What rule is difficult for you to follow when a guest teacher is in the classroom?

Fan-N-Pick

 7 Guest Teachers

What rule is easy for you to remember when a guest teacher is in the classroom?

Fan-N-Pick

 8 Guest Teachers

Pretend you are a guest teacher. Describe three student behaviors you would like to see during your visit in a classroom.

Fan-N-Pick

Management & Discipline: Activities Featuring Kagan Structures

Kagan Publishing • 800.933.2667 • www.KaganOnline.com

Guest Teachers

Fan-N-Pick Cards

Directions: Cut out each card along the dotted lines. Give each team a set of cards to play Fan-N-Pick.

9 **Guest Teachers**

Name two behaviors your teacher expects when a guest teacher is in the classroom.

Fan-N-Pick

10 **Guest Teachers**

Name two behaviors your teacher does NOT want to hear about when a guest teacher is in the classroom.

Fan-N-Pick

11 **Guest Teachers**

Name two ways you can show respect for a guest teacher.

Fan-N-Pick

12 **Guest Teachers**

Name two examples of responsible behavior a student could demonstrate when a guest teacher is in the classroom.

Fan-N-Pick

13 **Guest Teachers**

Name two examples of respectful behavior a student could demonstrate when a guest teacher is in the classroom.

Fan-N-Pick

14 **Guest Teachers**

What should the guest teacher see when it is time for him or her to teach? What should the guest teacher hear during teaching time?

Fan-N-Pick

15 **Guest Teachers**

What should the guest teacher see when it is time for silent work time? What should the guest teacher hear during silent work time?

Fan-N-Pick

16 **Guest Teachers**

Why should we treat guest teachers with respect?

Fan-N-Pick

Directions: Copy and cut out the Fan-N-Pick Mat along the dotted lines. Place the mat in the center of table to play Fan-N-Pick.

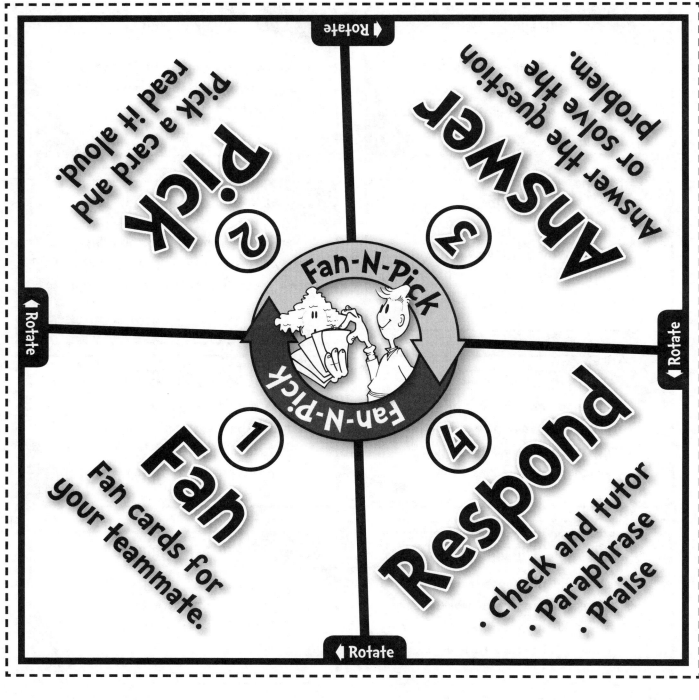

Rotate

Rotate

Rotate

Rotate

2 Pick
Pick a card and read it aloud.

3 Answer
Answer the question or solve the problem.

Fan-N-Pick

1 Fan
Fan cards for your teammate.

4 Respond
• Check and tutor
• Paraphrase
• Praise

Guest Teacher Expectations

Rappin' Teams

Purpose

- **To build relationships with teammates**
- **To review the expectations when a guest teacher is in the classroom**

Group Size

- Teams

Materials

- 1 Guest Teacher Expectations Key Words Recording Sheet per student
- 1 Guest Teacher Expectations Rap Rough Draft per team
- 1 Guest Teacher Expectations Our Final Team Rap worksheet per team
- 1 class timer
- 1 writing utensil per student

Preteaching

- Guest teacher expectations should have already been taught. This is a review activity.

Teacher   Preacher

Activity Overview

Teams develop a rap about behavior expectations for guest teachers.

Activity Steps

1 The teacher assigns the rap topic on guest teacher expectations.

2 Teammates use AllRecord RoundRobin to generate and record a list of eight key words on the Guest Teacher Expectations Key Words Recording Sheet provided.

3 Teammates use AllRecord RoundRobin to generate and record three or four rhyming words for each key word on the Guest Teacher Expectations Recording Sheet provided.

4 Using the key words, rhyming words, and meter, teammates work together to create lines for their rap using the Rap Rough Draft and then finalize using the Our Final Team Rap worksheet.

5 Teammates practice their rap, deciding roles for each teammate. For examples, which teammates will sing which lines, and which sound effects, clapping, or stomping.

6 Team up—teams perform their rap for another team.

Guest Teacher Expectations
Rappin' Teams Key Words Recording Sheet

Directions: Teams use this sheet to record the key words and rhyming words for each key word.

Key Words That Go with Classroom Rules	Rhyming Words
①	1. _____ 2. _____ 3. _____
②	1. _____ 2. _____ 3. _____
③	1. _____ 2. _____ 3. _____
④	1. _____ 2. _____ 3. _____
⑤	1. _____ 2. _____ 3. _____
⑥	1. _____ 2. _____ 3. _____
⑦	1. _____ 2. _____ 3. _____
⑧	1. _____ 2. _____ 3. _____

Management & Discipline: Activities Featuring Kagan Structures
Kagan Publishing • 800.933.2667 • www.KaganOnline.com

Guest Teacher Expectations

Rappin' Teams Rap Rough Draft

Directions: Teams use this sheet to create rough draft verses for their rap.

Team Rap Rough Draft

Rap Name _____

★**Key word:**_____
Rap verse using the key word and rhyming word(s):_____
_____
_____
_____

★**Key word:**_____
Rap verse using the key word and rhyming word(s):_____
_____
_____
_____

★**Key word:**_____
Rap verse using the key word and rhyming word(s):_____
_____
_____
_____

★**Key word:**_____
Rap verse using the key word and rhyming word(s):_____
_____
_____
_____

★**Key word:**_____
Rap verse using the key word and rhyming word(s):_____
_____
_____
_____

Guest Teacher Expectations

Rappin' Teams Our Final Team Rap

Directions: Teams use this worksheet to finalize and record their rap. When done writing their rap, they practice it as a team and prepare to perform it.

Team Rap Final Draft

Rap Name _____

_____

_____

_____

_____

_____

_____

_____

_____

_____

_____

_____

_____

_____

_____

_____

Kagan Publishing • 800.933.2667 • www.KaganOnline.com

Guest Teachers
Showdown

Purpose

- To increase positive behaviors when a guest teacher is in the building
- To teach and remind students what is expected when a guest teacher is in the building

Group Size

- Teams

Materials

- 1 set of Guest Teachers cards per team
- 1 "OK!" and 1 "Not OK!" response card per student

Preteaching

- Take a few minutes to review your classroom rules with everyone (see sample on page 158).
- Remind students the rules do not change if a guest teacher is present.

Activity Overview

Teams play Showdown to respond to questions about guest teachers. Students respond to each question with an "OK!" or "Not OK!" response card.

Activity Steps

1. The teacher selects one student on each team to be the Showdown Captain for the first round.

2. The Showdown Captain draws the top card, reads the statement about guest teachers to the team, and provides Think Time.

3. Students independently decide if the behavior is OK or not OK.

4. When finished, teammates signal they are ready by holding their selected response card against their chest.

5. The Showdown Captain calls, *"Showdown."*

6. Teammates show their response card and discuss why they chose "OK!" or "Not OK!"

7. The Showdown Captain leads the checking.

8. If correct, the team celebrates; if not, teammates tutor and then celebrate. If consensus can't be reached with the students, all four hands are raised and the teacher consults.

9. The person on the left of the Showdown Captain becomes the Showdown Captain for the next round.

Note: For younger students, the teacher can be the Showdown Captain and lead the group or class in Showdown.

Guest Teachers

Showdown Response Cards

Directions: Cut out each card along the dotted lines. Give each student one "OK!" and one "Not OK!" response card to play Showdown.

Guest Teachers

Showdown Cards

Directions: Cut out each card along the dotted lines. Give each team a set of cards to play Showdown.

---

① Guest Teachers

When the guest teacher leads the class in the hallway, all the students have their quiet reminders up.

Showdown

---

② Guest Teachers

During calendar time, everyone in the class has a quiet mouth and eyes on the calendar.

Showdown

---

③ Guest Teachers

Sally and Suzie keep trying to sneak and whisper to each other while the guest teacher is reading a story.

Showdown

---

④ Guest Teachers

The guest teacher asks a question and five students raise their hands to answer.

Showdown

---

⑤ Guest Teachers

Brianna shouts out answers when the teacher asks a question.

Showdown

---

⑥ Guest Teachers

The guest teacher asks the students where to find glue. All the students yell out the answer.

Showdown

Guest Teachers

Showdown Cards

Directions: Cut out each card along the dotted lines. Give each team a set of cards to play Showdown.

7 | **Guest Teachers**

At recess you see a guest teacher on duty. You ask him or her if you can play helicopter rope, even though you know it is against the school rules.

Showdown

8 | **Guest Teachers**

The guest teacher asks the class where to find extra paper. Julie raises her hand. She waits to be called on. Then she shows the guest teacher.

Showdown

9 | **Guest Teachers**

Mason runs in the hallway because he knows the guest teacher can't see him.

Showdown

10 | **Guest Teachers**

During silent work time, everyone is quietly working at his or her seat.

Showdown

11 | **Guest Teachers**

You ask the guest teacher if you can use markers on your math paper, even though you know your teacher's rule is crayons only.

Showdown

12 | **Guest Teachers**

When the guest teacher says her name, the kids in the class give her a smile.

Showdown

Guest Teachers

Showdown Cards

Directions: Cut out each card along the dotted lines. Give each team a set of cards to play Showdown.

 Guest Teachers

Mark wants to play a joke on the guest teacher. His friends tell him, *"No, that is a bad idea."* The rules are the same for teachers and guest teachers.

Showdown

 Guest Teachers

Bob asks the guest teacher 7 times if he can go the bathroom. He keeps asking even after the guest teacher said, *"No."*

Showdown

 Guest Teachers

The guest teacher tells the class she isn't happy about their behavior this morning. She says there has been too much talking. All the students try really hard to have quiet mouths in the afternoon.

Showdown

 Guest Teachers

The guest teacher asks Joe to take his seat. Joe does it right away.

Showdown

 Guest Teachers

When the guest teacher asks the students to line up, they get into line quickly and quietly.

Showdown

 Guest Teachers

The guest teacher accidently says your name wrong. You nicely say, *"My name is _____."*

Showdown

Guest Teachers
Showdown Blank Template

Directions: Use these blank cards to create your own Showdown Guest Teachers cards.

Teacher-Pleasing Behavior

Fan-N-Pick

Purpose

- To make sure all students understand expected classroom behavior

Group Size

- Teams

Materials

- 1 set of Teacher-Pleasing Behavior cards per team
- 1 Fan-N-Pick Mat per team (optional)

Preteaching

- Make sure students know classroom expectations.
- Review your classroom rules with the class (see sample on page 158).
- Go over the Teacher-Pleasing Behavior cards with the students. This activity is for review!

Activity Overview

Teammates play a card game to respond to questions or statements about teacher-pleasing behavior. Roles rotate with each new question or statement.

Activity Steps

1 Student #1 holds the Teacher-Pleasing Behavior cards in a fan and says, *"Pick a card, any card!"*

2 Student #2 picks a card, reads the question or statement aloud, and allows 5 seconds of Think Time.

3 Student #3 answers the question or statement about teacher-pleasing behavior.

4 Student #4 responds to the answer:
- For right or wrong answers, student #4 checks and then either praises or tutors.
- For questions that have no right or wrong answer, Student #4 does not check for correctness, but praises and then paraphrases the thinking that went into the answer.

5 Students rotate roles, one person clockwise for each new round.

Note: A Fan-N-Pick Mat can be placed in the center of the table to lead students through the structure, ensuring everyone keeps actively involved.

Structure Alternatives
- *Mix-Pair-Share*
- *Timed Pair Share*
- *StandUp-HandUp-PairUp*
- *Numbered Heads Together*

Teacher-Pleasing Behavior

Fan-N-Pick Cards

Directions: Cut out each card along the dotted lines. Give each team a set of cards to play Fan-N-Pick.

① **Teacher-Pleasing Behavior**

What should you do if your pencil breaks and you do not have another sharpened pencil at your desk?

Fan-N-Pick

② **Teacher-Pleasing Behavior**

Your shoulder partner is trying to talk to you while the teacher is talking. What should you do?

Fan-N-Pick

③ **Teacher-Pleasing Behavior**

You are taking a test and you have to go to the bathroom. What should you do?

Fan-N-Pick

④ **Teacher-Pleasing Behavior**

What should you do if you sneeze while the teacher is teaching and you need a tissue?

Fan-N-Pick

⑤ **Teacher-Pleasing Behavior**

Describe attentive behavior in a classroom setting.

Fan-N-Pick

⑥ **Teacher-Pleasing Behavior**

Your teacher is in the front of the classroom teaching at the board. Where should your eyes and your body be facing?

Fan-N-Pick

⑦ **Teacher-Pleasing Behavior**

What should you do when you finish your work and other students are still working?

Fan-N-Pick

⑧ **Teacher-Pleasing Behavior**

You are waiting in line for the bell to ring. What should you be doing?

Fan-N-Pick

Kagan Publishing • 800.933.2667 • www.KaganOnline.com

Teacher-Pleasing Behavior

Fan-N-Pick Blank Template

Directions: Use these blank cards to create your own Fan-N-Pick Teacher-Pleasing Behavior cards.

Teacher-Pleasing Behavior	Teacher-Pleasing Behavior
Fan-N-Pick	*Fan-N-Pick*
Teacher-Pleasing Behavior	Teacher-Pleasing Behavior
Fan-N-Pick	*Fan-N-Pick*
Teacher-Pleasing Behavior	Teacher-Pleasing Behavior
Fan-N-Pick	*Fan-N-Pick*
Teacher-Pleasing Behavior	Teacher-Pleasing Behavior
Fan-N-Pick	*Fan-N-Pick*

Teacher-Pleasing Behavior

Fan-N-Pick Mat

Directions: Copy and cut out the Fan-N-Pick Mat along the dotted lines. Place the mat in the center of table to play Fan-N-Pick.

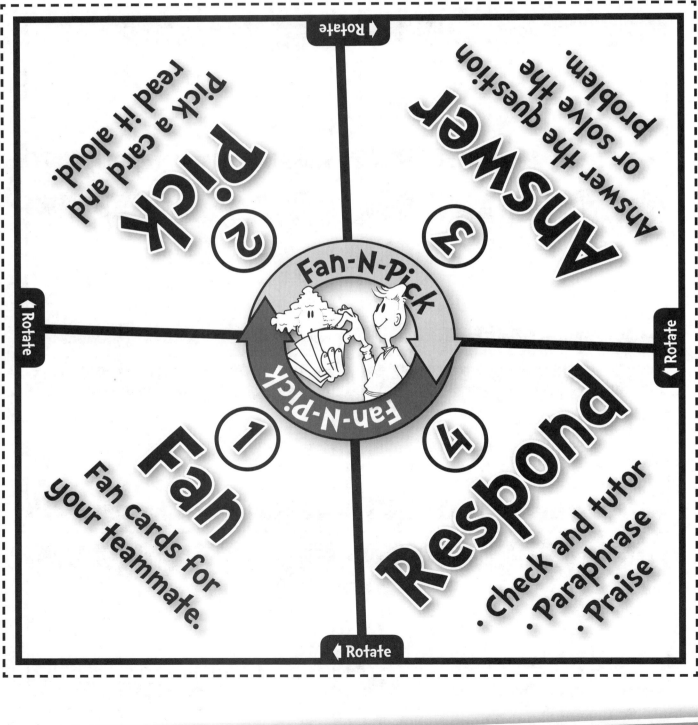

Rotate

② **Pick**
Pick a card and read it aloud.

③ **Answer**
Answer the question or solve the problem.

Rotate

Rotate

Fan-N-Pick

① **Fan**
Fan cards for your teammate.

④ **Respond**
· Check and tutor
· Paraphrase
· Praise

Rotate

Teacher-Pleasing Behavior

Fan-N-Pick Pairs

Purpose

- To review classroom rules with the students
- To ensure that all students know the classroom rules

Group Size

- Pairs

Materials

- 1 set of Teacher-Pleasing Behavior cards per pair
- 1 class timer

Preteaching

- Classroom rules should have already been taught before doing this activity (see sample on page 158).

Activity Overview

Partners play a card game to respond to questions about teacher-pleasing behavior. Roles rotate with each new question.

Activity Steps

1 Student #1 fans the Teacher-Pleasing Behavior cards and says, *"Pick a card, any card."*

2 Student #2 picks a card, reads the card aloud, and provides 5 seconds of Think Time.

3 Student #1 answers the question from the Teacher-Pleasing Behavior cards.

4 Student #2 restates what Student #1 said and then either praises if correct, or tutors if not correct.

5 Students switch roles for each new round.

Structure Alternatives
- *Fan-N-Pick (4 students)*
- *Quiz-Quiz-Trade*
- *Numbered Heads Together*

Teacher-Pleasing Behavior
Fan-N-Pick Pairs Cards

Directions: Cut out each card along the dotted lines. Give each pair a set of cards to play Fan-N-Pick Pairs.

 1 Teacher-Pleasing Behavior

You forgot to do your homework last night. What should you tell your teacher?

Fan-N-Pick Pairs

 2 Teacher-Pleasing Behavior

You need to sharpen your pencil. What should you do?

Fan-N-Pick Pairs

 3 Teacher-Pleasing Behavior

You forgot what to do when you were finished with your math. Who should you ask?

Fan-N-Pick Pairs

 4 Teacher-Pleasing Behavior

Kelly keeps talking to you in line when you are going to music class. Should you tell the teacher? What could you do?

Fan-N-Pick Pairs

 5 Teacher-Pleasing Behavior

You heard a classmate say some hurtful things to another classmate at recess. What should you do?

Fan-N-Pick Pairs

 6 Teacher-Pleasing Behavior

You need to use the bathroom, but the teacher is giving directions about your assignment. What should you do?

Fan-N-Pick Pairs

Management & Discipline: Activities Featuring Kagan Structures
Kagan Publishing • 800.933.2667 • www.KaganOnline.com

Teacher-Pleasing Behavior

Fan-N-Pick Pairs Cards

Directions: Cut out each card along the dotted lines. Give each pair a set of cards to play Fan-N-Pick Pairs.

 7 Teacher-Pleasing Behavior

You feel sick to your stomach because you didn't eat breakfast. What could you do?

Fan-N-Pick Pairs

 8 Teacher-Pleasing Behavior

Your neighbor is not working on the assignment, rather he or she is playing with a pencil. What could you do? Should you tell the teacher?

Fan-N-Pick Pairs

 9 Teacher-Pleasing Behavior

A classmate in your group came in late to school. The teacher already gave instructions and is now working with a group. What can you do to help?

Fan-N-Pick Pairs

 10 Teacher-Pleasing Behavior

You want to sit next to your friend on the carpet, but he or she is on the other side next to someone else. What should you do?

Fan-N-Pick Pairs

 11 Teacher-Pleasing Behavior

The teacher asks you to take out a pencil and paper, but you don't have any paper. What should you do?

Fan-N-Pick Pairs

 12 Teacher-Pleasing Behavior

The teacher gave instructions, but you are confused what to do next. What can you do?

Fan-N-Pick Pairs

Teacher-Pleasing Behavior

Showdown

Purpose

- **To make sure all students understand expected classroom behavior**

Group Size

- Teams

Materials

- 1 set of Teacher-Pleasing Behavior cards per team
- 1 "Happy" and 1 "Sad" response card per student

Preteaching

- Make sure students know teacher's expectations.
- Review classroom rules with your class (see sample on page 158).
- Go over the cards with the students (this activity is for review!).

Activity Overview

Teams play Showdown to respond to questions about teacher-pleasing behavior. Students respond to each question with a "Happy" or "Sad" response card.

Activity Steps

1. The teacher selects one student on each team to be the Showdown Captain for the first round.

2. The Showdown Captain draws the top card, reads the statement about teacher-pleasing behavior to the team, and provides Think Time.

3. Students independently decide if the behavior would make the teacher happy or sad.

4. When finished, teammates signal they are ready by holding their selected response card against their chest.

5. The Showdown Captain calls, *"Showdown."*

6. Teammates show their response card and discuss why they chose "Happy" or "Sad."

7. The Showdown Captain leads the checking.

8. If correct, the team celebrates; if not, teammates tutor, and then celebrate. If consensus can't be reached with the students, all four hands are raised and the teacher consults.

9. The person on the left of the Showdown Captain becomes the Showdown Captain for the next round.

Note: For younger students, the teacher can be the Showdown Captain and lead the group or class in Showdown.

Teacher-Pleasing Behavior

Showdown Response Cards

Directions: Cut out each card along the dotted lines. Give each student one "Happy" and one "Sad" response card to play Showdown.

Teacher-Pleasing Behavior
Showdown Cards

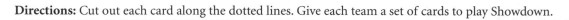

Directions: Cut out each card along the dotted lines. Give each team a set of cards to play Showdown.

 Teacher-Pleasing Behavior

Your pencil breaks. You do not have another sharpened pencil at your desk, and you scream out, *"Umm, my pencil broke!"*

Showdown

 Teacher-Pleasing Behavior

Your shoulder partner is trying to talk to you while the teacher is talking. You ignore him or her.

Showdown

 Teacher-Pleasing Behavior

You are taking a test and you have to go to the bathroom. You yell, *"I have to pee!!!,"* without raising your hand.

Showdown

 Teacher-Pleasing Behavior

You sneeze while the teacher is teaching and you need a tissue. You quietly walk over to the box of tissues, grab a tissue, wipe your nose, and throw the tissue away.

Showdown

 Teacher-Pleasing Behavior

You are sitting at the carpet on your bottom, legs crossed, mouth closed, and your eyes on the teacher.

Showdown

 Teacher-Pleasing Behavior

Your teacher is in the front of the classroom teaching at the board, your body is facing the back of the classroom and your eyes are on your friend.

Showdown

 Teacher-Pleasing Behavior

You finish your work and other students are still working. You yell out, *"I am done, what is taking everyone else so long?!"*

Showdown

 Teacher-Pleasing Behavior

You are waiting in line for the bell to ring with your mouth closed, your eyes straight ahead, and your hands at your side.

Showdown

Answer Key and School Charts

Management & Discipline
Answer Key

Section 1: Classroom Behavior

• Activity 1
• Answers will vary

• Activity 2: Classroom Disruptions
• *RoundTable (pp. 15–17)*

• **Page 15**
1. Quality Learning Environment
2. Disruption
3. Disruption
4. Quality Learning Environment
5. Disruption
6. Quality Learning Environment

• **Page 16**
7. Disruption
8. Disruption
9. Disruption
10. Disruption
11. Quality Learning Environment
12. Disruption

• **Page 17**
13. Quality Learning Environment
14. Disruption
15. Quality Learning Environment
16. Quality Learning Environment
17. Disruption
18. Disruption

• Activity 3
• Answers will vary

• Activity 4: Classroom Rules
• *Fact or Fiction (p. 25)*

1. Fact	2. Fiction
3. Fact	4. Fact
5. Fiction	6. Fiction
7. Fiction	8. Fiction

• Activity 5
• Answers will vary

Management & Discipline
Answer Key

Section 1: Classroom Behavior (continued)

• Activity 6: Classroom Behaviors
• Showdown (p. 33)

1. Not OK!	2. OK!
3. Not OK!	4. Not OK!
5. Not OK!	6. OK!
7. OK!	8. OK!

• Activity 7
• Answers will vary

• Activity 8: Compliance
• Showdown (pp. 41–42)

• Page 41		**• Page 42**	
1. Bigger	2. Smaller	7. Smaller	8. Smaller
3. Smaller	4. Bigger	9. Bigger	10. Smaller
5. Bigger	6. Smaller	11. Smaller	12. Bigger

Section 2: Schoolwide Rules

• Activity 10
• Answers will vary

• Activity 11: Bathroom Behavior
• Mix-Pair-Share (pp. 56–57)

• Page 56
1. In the garbage can.
2. Get in the bathroom, take care of business, and then get out.
3. Toilet flush.
4. Wash your hands.
5. (1) Wet your hands, (2) add soap, (3) wash, (4) rinse, and (5) dry.
6. Quiet voice.

• Page 57
7. Go into the bathroom when you need to use the toilet or sink. Stay out of the bathroom if you do not have a reason to go in. It is not an area for socializing.
8. Knock on the door or look under the stall for feet.
9. *"This stall is occupied,"* or *"I'm in here."*
10. Having someone not watch or bother you while using the bathroom.
11. Ask them to stop, and if necessary, alert the teacher.
12. It is never okay to hang out in the bathroom. The bathroom is for using the toilet or urinal, washing your hands, and then exiting.

Management & Discipline
Answer Key

Section 2: Schoolwide Rules (continued)

• Activity 12: Bathroom Behavior

• **Numbered Heads Together (p. 60)**

1. Get a teacher.
2. Put them in the garbage can.
3. Flush it yourself.
4. Answers will vary. (Your policy on bathroom use will determine it.)
5. The school matrix.
6. Hands to self, quiet mouth, quiet feet, and eyes watching for when it is his or her turn.
7. *"Excuse me,"* or *"I'm sorry."*

8. False. The bathroom is for using the toilet or urinal. Save your conversations for recess or lunch time.
9. • *"That's not safe."*
   • *"Stop."*
   • *"That's not a good choice."*
   • *"You are going to get in trouble."*
   • *"Don't do that."*
   • *"Remember the bathroom rules."*
10. One or two.

• Activity 14: Hallway Behavior

• **Showdown (pp. 75–76)**

• **Page 75**		• **Page 76**	
1. Not OK!	2. OK!	11. Not OK!	12. OK!
3. OK!	4. Not OK!	13. Not OK!	14. OK!
5. Not OK!	6. Not OK!	15. Not OK!	16. Not OK!
7. Not OK!	8. OK!	17. OK!	18. OK!
9. OK!	10. OK!	19. Not OK!	20. Not OK!

• Activities 15–27

• Answers will vary

Section 3: Recess Guidelines

• Activities 28–30

• Answers will vary

Management & Discipline
Answer Key

Section 4: Respecting Teachers

• Activities 32—33
- Answers will vary

• Activity 34: Guest Teachers
- *Showdown (pp. 137–139)*

  • Page 137
  1. OK!   2. OK!
  3. Not OK!   4. OK!
  5. Not OK!   6. Not OK!

  • Page 139
  13. OK!   14. Not OK!
  15. OK!   16. OK!
  17. OK!   18. OK!

  • Page 138
  7. Not OK!   8. OK!
  9. Not OK!   10. OK!
  11. Not OK!   12. OK!

• Activities 35—36
- Answers will vary

• Activity 37: Teacher-Pleasing Behavior
- *Showdown (p. 151)*
  1. Sad   2. Happy
  3. Sad   4. Happy
  5. Happy   6. Sad
  7. Sad   8. Happy

Classroom Rules

Sample Rules

Directions: You can use these sample Classroom Rules as a guide to develop your own classroom rules at the beginning of the school year. All students can agree on and are able to follow good classroom rules.

Classroom Rules

① Keep your hands and feet to yourself.

② Raise your hand and wait to be called on.

③ Pay attention when the teacher is talking.

④ Use quiet voices.

⑤ Follow the school rules.

⑥ HAVE FUN!!!!

Kagan Publishing • 800.933.2667 • www.KaganOnline.com

School Expectations

Sample Behavior Expectations

Directions: You can use this sample Behavior Expectations Chart as a guide to make up your own school rules. It is important that your school has clear and consistent rules for each common area in and around the buildings. This chart can also be called, "School Matrix," "School Rules," or "School Expectations."

Expectations	Hallways	Bathrooms	Cafeteria	Playground	Arrival	Dismissal	Stairs	Imaginarium	Assembly
Acknowledge	• Quiet zone • Walk in a line • Walk on the right • Be safe on the stairs	• Report problems • Use the facilities and supplies properly	• Talk at an appropriate voice level • Have appropriate conversations	• Be a good sport • Be kind • Include others • Take turns and share	• Be on time • Transition quietly	• Transition quietly	• Hands and feet to self	• Work together • Support peers • Encourage your peers to follow the rules	• Listen • Watch • Use appropriate applause
Accept Responsibility	• Eyes forward • Hands by your side • Keep personal space	• Flush • Trash in trash can	• Walk • Clean up after yourself	• Use equipment properly and return it • Be safe	• Walk • Be in the correct area	• Walk • Be in the correct area • Know your plan	• Use approved stairway • Be safe	• Be in your assigned area	• Enter and exit quietly • Sit in one spot
Comply	• Follow adult directions • Go straight to your destination	• Wash hands with soap and water • Leave it clean • Use time wisely • One stall per person	• Stay in your seat • Raise your hand for help	• Be a problem solver • Stay in your assigned area • Walk in quietly	• Follow adult directions • Be ready and pay attention	• Follow adult directions	• Be on task	• Be on task	• Enjoy the performance
Show Respect	• Respect property • Keep hands, feet, and objects to yourself	• Quiet zone • Wait your turn • Respect others' privacy • Respect property • Be responsible	• Good manners • Hands to self • Be kind • Respect property	• Good manners • Follow adult directions • Stop playing when signaled and line up	• Keep personal space • Good manners	• Keep personal space	• Talk at an appropriate voice level • Respect property	• Follow adult directions • Respect property	• Keep personal space

Management & Discipline
Notes

Management & Discipline
Notes

Management & Discipline
Notes

Management & Discipline
Notes

Management & Discipline
Notes

Management & Discipline: Activities Featuring Kagan Structures
Kagan Publishing • 800.933.2667 • www.KaganOnline.com

Management & Discipline
Notes

166 Management & Discipline: Activities Featuring Kagan Structures
Kagan Publishing • 800.933.2667 • www.KaganOnline.com